# Class Acts

## DRAMA FOR JUNIOR CERTIFICATE

Carmen Cullen

FOLENS

Printed in Ireland at the press of the publishers

© Folens Publishers
Unit 7 Broomhill Business Park
Tallaght
Dublin 24

ISBN: 0 86121 5850

Editor: Anna O'Donovan

Design/Typesetting: Anne Lewis

All rights reserved. No part of this publication may be reproduced or transmitted in any form or by any means (stencilling, photocopying, etc.) for whatever purpose, even purely educational without written permission from the publisher.

The publisher reserves the right to change, without notice at any time the specification of this product, whether by change of materials, colours, bindings, format, text revision or any other characteristic.

# Contents

| | |
|---|---|
| Introduction | vii |
| Leaving Home – 1 | 1 |
| Leaving Home – 2 | 3 |
| A Dream School – 1 | 4 |
| A Dream School – 2 | 5 |
| Babysitting | 7 |
| Going Shopping | 10 |
| Aliens – 1 | 12 |
| Aliens – 2 | 14 |
| Van Dieman's Land – 1 | 17 |
| Van Dieman's Land – 2 | 20 |
| Service, Please! | 22 |
| Odd One Out | 26 |
| The Kiss of Life | 34 |
| The Wolf | 45 |
| A First Confession | 49 |
| Not My Best Friend | 62 |
| The Slumber Party | 76 |

# Introduction

Though we might not think about it very much, drama has now become part of our everyday lives. I am referring, of course, to films as drama and television and stage plays.

Films are by their nature dramatic. Drama on television can cover many fields, ranging from stage to serials. Both are based on the same principal, the use of a script to provide entertainment for an audience.

Stage plays brings us closer to the idea of drama. The main difference is their use of live performance, the presence of actors on the stage before us. So close do we feel to the action, for a while it seems we are belonging with the actors in their stage lives. We get to know their hopes and fears. By becoming emotionally involved with them we know what it is like to feel as their characters feel on stage. From this experience we have fresh insights into the emotions of our own lives.

In this drama book you are asked to imagine your classroom as a stage with you, the students, as actors on it. A good story or plot is essential to the success of any play. Your play will depend on how you as actors put your story across. You will also learn about other aspects of production such as directing, set design, use of props, sound, costumes, lights and so on.

The first section of the book gently introduces you to the idea of acting. It begins by giving you play themes to work on and drama activities related to these themes. You will be asked to assume a character. At first, your character might be sitting down. Later on you and whoever you are acting with can stand up and walk around. This need not be attempted until you have built up your own self-confidence. Active involvement in drama in this way will teach you about the demands of staging and the difficulties of putting across a piece of acting to an audience.

The second half of the book provides you with completed play-scripts. Because you have now become used to creating a character you will find it easier to play the part of a character in a script. You will also have learnt something about production techniques. This experience will help you take on the more extensive production requirements of a scripted play.

Each unit of the book is supplied with writing assignments. One of the functions of these is to allow you to write dialogue. Suggested ideas for dialogue are directly linked to the drama activities given in the units. Ideas for other plays are included as well. There are questions on the texts to give you a better understanding of the plays and production notes for their staging. Writing around and about the plays will help you, should you take one of them as your choice for the Junior Cert.

The aim of this book is to help you answer the modern drama section on the English paper for the Junior Cert. By asking you to participate in drama in the classroom it gives you a better understanding of how plays are written, directed and performed. Being familiar with this approach will give you a different outlook on any other play you might read, see or choose to study for the Junior Cert.

Carmen Cullen

# Leaving Home
## -1-

We begin our first play by asking you, the student, to imagine you are an actor. Imagine too, your classroom is a stage, and you and all of your class are the actors on it. In the following play, everyone in the class will be taking part. From now on, when you are on stage (in your classroom), whether you are talking or not, you are an actor.

In this first play the stage is a hall where a group of people have gathered. Imagine your classroom as this hall. It has windows and doors. It also has a blackboard. On the board are written the words "Selection Meeting. 8 p.m." Sit in your place and wait. You are these people.

This is the year 3,000AD. Many changes have taken place on earth – in technology, the clothes people wear, the food they eat and so on. Even so there are still rich and poor, governments, schools and different social groupings. A number of climatic and gravitational changes have taken place as well and small settlements have been started on other planets.

Something has gone badly wrong on earth and nobody is quite sure what it might mean for the survival of the human race. For the last while the sun has been behaving erratically. It has been travelling closer to the earth. Scientists are monitoring the situation.

People stay indoors and watch. The sun hangs like a ball of fire. This is an emergency. At last the government acts and your meeting is arranged to take place.

## The Meeting

It is eight o'clock and a representative of the government (acted by your teacher), arrives. 'Ladies and Gentlemen,' begins the representative, 'thank you all for coming. In response to our present crisis, on behalf of the government I would like to make the following announcement. Arrangements are being made to ferry as many of you as possible to another planet. Everyone has a right to go.' To make sure you can you must complete the following exercises:

*Class Acts*

 **Drama Activities** *(Each member of the class is to complete the 3 activities)*

1. Give your name age and date of birth.

2. Mime an activity connected to a job you would like to do, for your life on this planet. (Let the class guess the mime.)

3. Like Noah's Ark, you will all be allowed bring one pair of birds or animals with you. Give the class **20 guesses** to help them find out what each person's choice is.

After this meeting the representative declares that you will be informed in writing, if you are allowed to go.

 **Writing Assignment**

Write a letter to the Governor of the planet to which you are going. Give information about yourself, your age, schooling, interests, personality and so on.

# Leaving Home
## - 2 -

The threat to the planet Earth continues; the sun is still hanging like a sulphorous mass in the sky. Conflicting arguments rage about what the future holds. Some say the sun will gradually recede, others that the destruction of the earth is inevitable. Just when it seems all is lost, some hope for optimism begins to filter through. A top secret investigation has revealed that though it will continue its downward spiral and the surface of the earth will become badly scorched, the sun will not fall.

The Irish government finds out and to help people who are left behind, decides to build bunkers for its most important citizens. There is immediate uproar. Ordinary people complain that they are being left out. After much pressure the government finally agrees to let others take part.

Your class have now become the group who are applying to go into the bunkers. You will be allowed to go if you are successful in the following activities.

## Drama Activities *(Each member of the class is to take part in both activities)*

1. (a) Pick any famous person you like, in Ireland or abroad. Pretend you are this person and let the class play the game **20 questions** with you. If they can guess who you are you will be allowed go into a bunker. (**20 Questions:** Each member of the class, up to 20, has the right to ask one question, to guess the identity of the famous person. The only answer they may be given is "yes" or "no".)

2. You are allowed bring an item with you which you feel will be of use in the bunker. Mime an activity connected with this item and let the class guess what it is.

## Writing Assignments

1. Write a letter of application from a famous person explaining why he/she should be allowed to go to a bunker.

2. Write a letter of application from an ordinary person to the government explaining why he/she should be allowed go to a bunker.

# A Dream School
## - 1 -

Imagine going into school one day to be told your school is being closed down! People in business suits have been walking around the school in small groups for some time now, peering into this room and that and talking in low voices. Nobody bothers to tell you what is going on. Explanations have been vague, there is a rumour circulating about your school being used to host an International Youth Conference.

Soon rumours abound. You are going to be sent abroad to another school for a week while the conference takes place. It is to be a specialist school of your own choice, dealing with what you like to do best, such as music, sport, acting or dancing and so on. This would indeed be the chance of a lifetime. You know rumour has become fact when you are presented with an exciting list of schools from which you can choose.

The day arrives when you are going to be allowed to talk about your choice. You are the actor on the stage and once more the play is taking place in your classroom. All participants have to take part in the following preparations.

### Drama Activities *(Each member of the class is to take part in both activities)*

1. Stand up, give your name and age and your choice and location of specialist school saying why you want to go there.

2. When you arrive at your destination abroad you will be allocated a house to stay. You know the occupation of one member of this household. Mime this occupation for the class and see if they can guess it. No two students can mine the same occupation.

### Writing Assignments

Write a prose passage, story or poem on one of the following:
1. School.
2. My Dream School.

# A Dream School
## - 2 -

In part one of this play you were allocated a school and a household to stay in, somewhere abroad. Now you have arrived. You are immediately presented with some problems. What these problems are and how you deal with them are the subject of your next acting parts. Until you get used to acting, if you would prefer to just sit down and talk your way through the part you can do so. You can keep your scene as short as 30 seconds or as long as you want. Make a part of the classroom your stage. Read the following suggestions and take a few minutes to prepare them.

 **Drama Activities**

1. You are asked to stay with a farmer living on his own. He is a man of about 60 who, up to now, has only had a dog for company. He is not used to having a young person around and treats you as he was treated when he was young. For example, you have to go to bed at eight o'clock. He also expects you to go for long walks with him and the dog. You have made friends with a person of your age in the school who has asked you to go to a film in the town in the evening. The old man disagrees. Conversation between you and the old man. (Two students)

2. You are asked to stay with a family who has somebody there who is the same age as you. You both get on very well. One day you decide to go and see the sights in town instead of going to school. Whose fault is this? Conversation between you, your friend and the mother of your friend. (Three students)

3. The mother and father in the house where you have been asked to go and stay have been killed in a car-crash. An older brother and sister are in charge. Everybody in the house has their own jobs except you, because you are a visitor. One of the younger children in the house complains and says you should do some work too. Conversation between the older brother or sister and the younger one first, and with you afterwards. (Three students)

4. You are staying with a family and find a watch which you thought you had lost, in the bag of one of the children. You're not sure if it was stolen, so you just take it back. The next day you find some of your Irish money in the same

bag. You tell the person's father or mother. Conversations between you, the parent and the other child. (Three students)

5. You are staying with a very cross person. You break something belonging to them. (Two students)

6. A policeman comes to the door of the house in which you are staying. He is there to arrest a young person in the house with whom you have become friendly, for joy-riding. He used to be involved in this crime before but on this occasion he was with you. You have to convince the policeman of this. There will be language difficulties because the policeman's English is not very good. (Three students)

7. You have been staying with a family who are not feeding you properly, even though they have been given money from the government to do so. Conversations between you, a teacher you complain to and the mother or father in the house in which you are staying. (Three students)

8. You have been invited to stay with the family you are residing with for another month. You would like to do this because you all get along very well. You are also needed at home to study for an exam. Phone home. Conversation between you and your mother/father. (Two students)

9. You support one football team and your friend supports another. Discuss the merits of each one as rival supporters. An alternative conversation would be their country versus yours, or your favourite T.V. programme versus the other person's and so on. (Two students)

 ## Writing Assignments

1. Write a story, poem or essay piece on one of the following:
    (1) Holidays.
    (2) Going Abroad.
    (3) Not wanted here.

2. Write a letter home or to a friend from a holiday abroad telling about some unusual experience you had while away.

# Babysitting

Every student has been involved in babysitting at some time. But the circumstances surrounding this case of babysitting are unusual.

The story begins when the people you regularly babysit for come and tell you there has been a crisis in the family. The mother is seriously ill in hospital in Belfast. Nobody has been prepared for this but they must go there straight away. It is Thursday evening. They feel they might be away for three days. They have twins aged nine. It is June and you are on your holidays but the twins are not. Will you babysit? If you can they would like to offer you £50.

This is an opportunity you don't want to turn down. You have to consult with your parents. You admit the twins can be a handful but hope to be able to call on your parents' help if necessary. Eventually they agree and you ring back and accept the offer to babysit.

During your stay in the house a number of situations occur which you have to deal with. Read the following situations carefully and pick a point you may act or speak about (sitting down). Think about the character you are supposed to be and put some feeling into the part.

## Drama Activities

1. It is nine o'clock. One of the children has gone to bed but the other refuses to go. She wants to stay up and watch a programme on television which ends at ten o'clock. You don't agree with this. You think she is too young to stay up and you tell her so. There is an argument. (Two students)

2. You have been left some money to buy shopping for the dinner on Saturday. You buy some pieces of chicken in a butcher. When you get home you discover that one is bad. You know the sale of bad meat should not be allowed. You go back to the butcher to complain but he will not accept your story. Have an argument. (Two students)

# Class Acts

3. On Friday morning one of the twins is very sick and cannot go to school. The other twin refuses to go as well. You feel the second twin is acting unfairly. Argument between yourself and the healthy twin. (Two students)

4. The teacher arrives at the door on Friday afternoon. She says that one of the twins has been missing all day. You discuss this with the twins afterwards and find that one has been mitching. You disagree with her action. An argument develops. (Three students)

5. On Friday night your friend arrives and asks you to go to a disco as it is your birthday. You say you have to babysit. The twins have been asleep for some time and you know they won't wake up. The disco is only five minutes down the road. All your friends will be there. Your friend tries to persuade you. You can't agree. Does she succeed? (Two students)

6. The twins throw their books and games on the sitting-room floor and then sit down to watch television. You don't like this and say the television has to stay off until the room has been tidied. (Three students)

7. It is Saturday. The twins have gone down to a friend's house to play for an hour. It is now three hours later and they haven't returned. You ring up the house and they are not there. Eventually they arrive home at six o'clock. You are very annoyed with them because you consider this to be irresponsible. Argument. (Three students)

8. One of the twins has taken the other's toy. They fight over this. You think they are behaving badly. You have to settle the dispute. (Three students)

9. One of the twins has broken a glass bowl in the sitting-room. You want to find out what has happened and who is responsible because you feel they should own up. Also you want to be able to tell their parents in case you get blamed. (Three students)

10. You have a few friends over and have a party on Saturday night. The parents arrive home early on Sunday morning and the house is a mess. They don't want to give you the £50. You know you are in the wrong, yet you decide to argue your own case. (Three students)

**Writing Assignments**

1. (a) Write out one of the series of conversations you have just heard in dialogue form.
    
    **or**
    
    (b) Write your own piece of dialogue on a similar theme.

2. Write a prose piece, story or poem on one of the following:
   (a) Lost.
   (b) Grown-ups.
   (c) An unexpected windfall.

# Going Shopping

Each person in the class has £100 to spend and it's all thanks to the President of Ireland.

The whole affair began when you and your class were involved in doing a nature project on the Phoenix Park in Dublin. To your great surprise you were allowed a visit to Áras an Uachtaráin. Back at school, work on the projects progressed smoothly. When they were finished a selection of them was sent as a thank-you gesture to the President. To your delight a letter arrived in your school one day addressed to all your class. It was from the President. Your teacher read it out, it said, in response to receiving the projects, that the President wished to pay your school, and your class in particular, the honour of a visit.

This was great news. The school was *en fête* and you were looking your best when the President arrived. Speeches were made. Finally the President said she had her own award to make. All the students in your class were to be given £100 each for their involvement in doing the projects. Because it was a single award, the President added, the entire £100 was to be spent in one day. The next day the class went into town for their day's shopping. During the course of the day a number of situations occurred that had to be dealt with. Allocate the parts for these, then put some time into the preparation of your scenes.

## Drama Activities

1. You go up to a check-out assistant with a bundle of clothes in your hand. She or he checks them through. When this is all done you search for your money. You discover you have left it at home. Talk or act out the conversation between both of you. (Two students)

2. You bought a radio-cassette recorder. When you get home you discover it does not work. You have lost the receipt. When you bring it back to the shop they are not interested in taking it back. Talk or act out what happens. (Two students)

3. You see something in a shop (a bike!) that costs £120. You bargain with the seller to try and bring the price down to £100. (Two students)

## Going Shopping

4. You want to buy a present for your mother out of the £100. You want it to be a surprise but she says she is coming into town to help you to do your shopping. Try and persuade her not to. (Two students)

5. You go to the bank to cash the cheque before going into town. The cashier refuses to believe you could have a cheque signed by the President of Ireland. A discussion follows. (Two students)

6. You have been warned by your parents not to spend all of the £100 on one item. You, however against their wishes, buy a guitar worth £100. When you go home your father or mother tells you that you had no right to do it and order you to bring it back to the shop. (Two students)

7. Your friend comes along and asks you to lend her £30 for a new jacket. She says she will give you her birthday money the following Saturday. You don't want to do this. (Two students)

8. During the course of your shopping, in one department store you are robbed of the £100. Conversation between the security guard and you about what happened and what can be done about it. (Two students)

9. You were given a cheque for £150 by mistake. You cash this and spend it. When you get home you are accused of stealing some of the things you bought. Act out a conversation between you and your parent. (Two students)

10. When you get to the check-out the security guard comes up and accuses you of stealing the £100. You have been found shoplifting in this shop before. Now you have to prove the money is really yours. What happens? (Two students)

11. Your mother or father tries to persuade you to lodge some of the money in the bank. You don't want to. (Two students)

12. You pretend your cheque for £100 has been stolen from your house when it was burgled. In reality, you have lost it. Ring up the President's office and lie in order to try and get another cheque. Do you get found out? (Two students)

### Writing Assignments

1. Write out your version of one of the pieces of dialogue.
   **or**
   Write a piece of dialogue between two characters on your own or a similar theme.

2. Write a letter to the President to thank her, explaining how you spent the money and showing your appreciation of her visit to the school.

# Aliens
## - 1 -

We are travelling once more into the future. The year is 2,050 and great advances in space exploration have taken place. Stars in other galaxies have been explored and the information brought back to earth. A surprise discovery is made. A new planet is discovered in space and it is inhabited.

News travels quickly. Inhabitants of this planet it seems, have a civilisation superior to ours. They have been keeping a close eye on us all this time and they consider us to be barbarians. They are not so sure they want us to continue to visit them. This is an unexpected development. Nevertheless, talks begin to take place between the two races.

Inhabitants of the planet are green in colour. They have willowy bodies that ripple like seaweed. They become known to us as The Green People. You are told that some of the people on their planet who are not well educated might have a prejudice against us on earth because of the colour of our skin.

At long last they agree to let a group of us visit their planet to inform them about our daily life on earth.

This is your play and you are the group of people who have been chosen to go on this mission. A spokesperson for The Green People arrives on earth. Let your teacher play this part. The following activities must be performed.

## Drama Activities

1. Each one of you gives your name and some piece of information about yourself to The Green Person. You then explain why you think it is a good idea that you be sent to the planet.

2. Because of language difficulties, you are told there might be problems with humans being understood on the planet. You will have to use sign language. Think of some daily need or activity in your own lives. (Mime this activity) If the class can guess what it is you will be allowed to go. Each one of you must have your own mime.

**Writing Assignments**

1. Write a description of what you think the visiting alien on earth looks like.
   **or**
   A description given by an alien in their report, of a human.

2. A story, poem or prose on one of the following:
   1. The stars.
   2. Prejudice.
   3. Getting away from home.

# Aliens

## – 2 –

The entire class arrives on the planet. It is a sunny day but the air has a lavender tinge. The welcoming party waves before you like shimmering trees. In the distance is a ring of orange mountains. The aliens, as you think of them, fly about in bubble craft. A fleet of these is going to ferry you to your hotel for your first night.

Their buildings are different. All the rooms are on the outside as though hooked to a pole. Their language sounds like singing. There are no roads because all travel is by air but there are streets and shops with special landing places.

Your trip to the hotel is pleasant. When you arrive each of you is allocated a bodyguard, in case of attack by any Green People who might dislike the way you look. Breakfast arrives the next morning but you have been served a four-course dinner. It is with great difficulty that you manage to explain their mistake!

During the course of your stay on this planet a number of situations occur which you have to deal with. Talk or act out these situations.

## 🎭 Drama Activities

1. You want to see what sweets are like on this planet. You have been told not to go out without your escort but you do so. When you get to a shop two aliens stop you and question you about going inside. They don't like the "colour of your skin". (Three students)

2. During your stay on the planet, after your first night in the hotel, you go and stay with a family. The mother or father of the family explains to the son/daughter about who is coming and why. The child doesn't like the idea. (Two students)

3. You arrive at the house of a family. Shortly afterwards one of the children starts to steal things from you, first a wallet with pictures of your family and then a walkman. You go to the father or mother and explain what's happening. The child denies it. Who do they believe? (Three students)

4. You have to visit a classroom where two students ask you questions about earth. They are complaining about it to you; about fighting, pollution, no jobs, people starving, etc. You have to defend your planet. (Three students)

5. You are walking down the street and somebody plants drugs on you. A green policeman sees what is happening and arrests you for possession. He believes you were buying the drug. You have to argue your own defence. He doesn't like humans. (Two students)

6. You are a boy from the planet Earth. You fall in love with an alien girl. Though she is different from you she is very beautiful. She asks her mother can she go out with you but her mother refuses. The girl goes back and tells you what happens and you both decide what to do. (Three students)

7. One of your group goes to the president of the planet to say you want to stay on the planet to live. The president agrees, but on a number of conditions. Discussion between you and the president. (Two students)

8. To prove to themselves that human beings can have their practical uses the aliens ask you to do some work. One of you has been ordered to clean all the floors of their buildings. You refuse to do this. Conversation between you and the alien who asks you what is wrong with this request. (Two students)

9. Another one of you is given the job of serving in a café. Two aliens come in and start ordering you around. You don't like this and complain to the manager. (Four students)

## Writing Assignments

1. A conversation between two aliens about these humans who have come to visit.
   **or**
   A description in your own words of this or a similar planet visited by humans

2. (a) A letter home describing your experiences.
   **or**
   (b) An unexpected adventure on the planet of the Green People.

3. Read the following information and answer the question on it.

## Stage Plan

Plays can be performed anywhere so long as you have an audience. A stage has only three walls, the back and two sides. The fourth wall disappears so the actors can look out at the audience. Look at your classroom. Decide where the back and two sides are and which wall will disappear. Know how you get on or off the stage.

Stand in the middle of your classroom stage. You are centre stage. In front of you is *stage front*. Behind you is *backstage*. To your right is *stage right* and to your left is *stage left*. Identify your *exit* and *entrance* points.

At all times during a play, you or the other actors will be standing, sitting or moving in one of these areas.

## Diagram of a Stage Plan

| Backstage Left | | Backstage Right |
|---|---|---|
| Stage Left | Centre Stage | Stage Right |
| Front Stage Left | | Front Stage Right |

## The Stage Set

On the stage is some furniture. Furniture on a play stage is known as *props*. The props will indicate where your play is set; in a kitchen, on the street, in the shop and so on. This furniture or fittings on a stage make up the *stage set*.

 **Question**

List six props (large or small) which you think should be on stage for the following locations.
1. A kitchen
2. A bedroom
3. A doctor's surgery

# Van Dieman's Land
## - 1 -

A court-room scene is about to take place in your classroom and you, the students, are the actors who are going to take part. There will be a judge but no jury. You will be asked to step forward and plead your own case. Each one of you must adopt an identity and invent a crime of which you are to be accused.

In Ireland, in the last century, people could be either hanged, fined or deported for committing a crime. Deportation was a very popular method used for punishment. It was also a handy way of getting rid of people convicted of treason or disagreeing with the Crown. This way of dealing with crime was not just used for the Irish but for people in England and the rest of Britain as well. Most crimes for which people were deported were of a simple nature, like stealing small amounts of money or fighting. Of course, murderers and more serious criminals were also convicted. Whatever the crime, they were all given the same sentence of deportation. The descendants of these people later helped to colonise Australia. The place they were sent to was Van Dieman's Land off the southern coast of that continent.

## Drama Activities

1. **Court-room Drama**
   The judge, who is the teacher or another student, calls out each of your names in turn and asks you to step forward and state the nature of the crime of which you have been accused. You all do this and plead your own cause. Nobody wishes to be convicted and everyone should offer a very good self-defence.

   Though in many cases it is obvious you are innocent and the judge is acting unfairly, the entire class is convicted of their crimes.

2. **After the Trial**
   The class is to go to Van Dieman's Land. Before the voyage and during it a number of situations arise which you, as the people involved, will have to handle. A difficulty that arises is that many of you, though found guilty, are in fact not and have lived honest lives. You will have to adopt a variety of roles during these situations.

## Class Acts

1. You don't want to go because you know your mother is sick and can't cope on her own. You have to go to the magistrate and ask if you would be allowed to stay. (Two students)

2. Although convicted, you manage to escape from jail in Ireland before leaving for Van Dieman's Land. You go home to your own house to collect some possessions before going into hiding. A policeman arrives as you are in the house. You hide upstairs. Your mother and father have to persuade the policeman that you are not there and that he need not search the house. (Three students)

3. You have some money saved and you want a suit made for yourself for the voyage. A tailor comes into the Irish jail. You have to bargain with him about the price. (Two students)

4. You want a friend to come with you but you will have to smuggle him on board. Try and persuade him to come. (Two students)

5. During the course of the voyage you find out that one of the passengers is sick with a killer, infectious disease. You go to the ship's captain to warn him and ask him to do something. He doesn't care. How do you try to convince him? (Two students)

6. You are a mother and father both convicted of a crime. Though told you could not do this, you have smuggled your child on board. The ship's captain finds out and tells you he will be bringing the child back with him on the return voyage, or dropping him/her off at their next port of call. You have to plead with the captain for your child. How can you convince the captain? (Three students)

7. You are a sneaky type and find out there is a mutiny planned. You won't give the captain details of this unless he promises to release you. (Two students)

8. You refuse to eat the ship's food and the cook calls the captain. Argue your point with both. (Three students)

9. There is a fight on board the ship. Both of the people involved have been sentenced to be thrown overboard. You have been asked by the others to plead their case. There is a danger that your intervention might be seen as a crime too! (Three students)

10. Two brothers or a brother and sister, have been together since the start of the voyage. When they arrive one is told that there is a mistake and that one is

being allowed home. Each one tries to persuade the other to stay at home and let them go. (Two students)

## Writing Assignments

1. A report for a radical Irish newspaper on the trials.

2. A week's entry in a diary by someone who is on the voyage to Van Dieman's Land.

3. A story, poem or prose essay on one of the following titles:
   a) Emigration.
   b) Leaving Home.
   c) Going abroad for the first time.

# Van Dieman's Land

## - 2 -

When you arrive in Van Dieman's Land you are all put in prison. Most of the buildings are crude huts. The countryside around is dangerous and if you escape you will probably be killed by natives. You are all sentenced to hard labour. Your diet is very poor and the conditions in the huts are bad. Even though your work is back-breaking the climate of the country you are in is good and it is very beautiful. Many of you are severely affected by the conditions in the prison. After a while some of you plan an escape. The following situations take place. Talk or act out these situations.

 **Drama Activities**

1. You are put into the hen's hut. You go and complain to the Governor. The Governor doesn't care. (Two students)

2. When you arrive you have been elected by those on the voyage to go and tell the Governor about you as a group, your skills and what work you feel you can do. Instead of listening he gives you the rules of the prison. You argue that your group could be more constructively employed while in prison. (Two students)

3. During each afternoon you have a one-hour recreation period. You want to organise a football match. Somebody else wants to organise athletics or perhaps put on a play. Argue both cases. (Two students)

4. You are a guard. You overhear a conversation about a plan to murder the prison Governor. You bring one of the people involved before the Governor and try to get him to admit to what you have heard. The Governor next summonses a friend of the accused and tries to persuade him that the accused has admitted to being guilty and that therefore he should own up. Argue both cases. (Four students)

5. You go to the Governor of the jail and ask him for an early release for good behaviour. He doesn't want to grant it. (Two students)

6. When an escape is being planned one of the prisoners gets very sick. Two of

the others have a discussion. One says it would be dangerous to bring the sick prisoner, the other says it would be wrong to leave him behind. One of you has to go back and give your decision to the sick prisoner. (Three students)

7. One of the Scottish prisoners overhears your plan. You have to convince him not to tell on you. If he does he will probably get released. (Two students)

8. An Irish prisoner does not want to come with you. She knows she will be released in a few years time and she prefers to stay, rather than risk getting caught. One of the others has to try and convince her to come, since she knows the plan and might tell the guards if questioned. (Two students)

9. Three groups of two work out separate plans of escape. They have to explain their plans to the group of prisoners. The rest of the prisoners vote on which is the best plan to follow. (Six students and class voting)

10. One of the prisoners from the English group has been sentenced to be hanged for murder on the day after your planned escape. Some of the Irish prisoners believe he murdered the guard in question. Some believe he did not. He asks the leaders of the Irish group to be allowed to plead his case to escape with them. They agree. He comes before them. Should the Irish group allow him to escape with them? (One student as the English prisoner and the rest of the class as the planned escapees, discuss the case.)

## Writing Assignments

1. Describe the stage set, including the position of the furniture, where one of the drama situations takes place.

2. Write out the dialogue for one of the situations you have acted in or another conversation with a similar theme.

3. Write an essay, story or poem on one of the following:
   a) The Prisoner.
   b) Teenage Crime.
   c) Escape.

# Service, Please!

## A short play for schools

CHARACTERS
Old man
Cafe waitress
Two young men (Michael and Gary)
Gang of three (Darren, Decko and Steve)

SCENE
A Café

Old man walks into café and sits down. He is using a walking stick. He places this beside him. Waitress walks down towards him. She has a pad in her hand. She stands over the old man. *(Old man enters backstage right and walks to front stage centre. Sits. Waitress moves from backstage left to old man)*

OLD MAN: Can I see the menu please?

WAITRESS: Oh sorry! (She goes and gets one) Here it is. *(Waitress walks back to desk, backstage left and then to old man)*

OLD MAN: (Studies menu) What's your lunch special today?

WAITRESS: It's nice. Vegetable soup and roast chicken and apple tart. It's not re-heated or anything.

OLD MAN: That sounds nice. I'll have that.

WAITRESS: Right.

Three young men come into the café: Darren, Decko and Steve. They look around them before sitting down. Darren goes up to the old man. *(Young man moves to front stage left)*

DARREN: Here lads. Sit here.

DECKO: Beside him? He's dirty. Look. There's fleas crawling all over him.

STEVE: We could ask the waitress to fry them.

DARREN: Yea right! (laughs) Hey, auld fella, do you mind if we sit here?

OLD MAN: I'd prefer not to be disturbed, if you don't mind.

DECKO: Disturbed? You're what's disturbed around here. Give us a few bob, will ya?

STEVE: Him? He wouldn't give you anything. Look at the state of him. You'd have to rob him to get anything off him. Did anyone ever rob ya, did they mister? Where's your gaff?

DARREN: We'll get him outside. (He points to table in corner) Here. Sit down before the waitress comes up. That waitress is a nosy parker. She lives on my road. We'll have to plan this. I bet he has a load of money in his pocket. (Waitress comes up and stands over them) *(Waitress comes to the table from backstage left)*

DECKO: A pot of tea for three and one bun.

WAITRESS: Who's paying for this?

STEVE: I'm paying. Now get the stuff over here. Pronto.

Two young men, Gary and Michael enter. They go and sit at a separate table. The waitress comes down to sit by them. The other three have started to smoke and put their feet up. *(Gary and Michael move to front stage right and sit down)*

WAITRESS: (standing beside the table of the two newcomers) Can I help you?

MICHAEL: Coffee for two please. And I'll have a salad sandwich.

GARY: Do you have chips on their own?

WAITRESS: I don't know. I think they're only served with a meal. Hold on and I'll find out. (She goes)

GARY: (Looking at "The Lads") There's no smoking here.

STEVE: Here, what's wrong with you? We'll smoke if we want to.

MICHAEL: My friend is right. The sign on the wall over your head says, "No Smoking". Would you mind putting the cigarette out?

DECKO: Do you hear him? Get stuffed, mate.

# Class Acts

DARREN: (Mimicking) You don't own the place you know.

MICHAEL: If you don't put out the cigarette I'm calling the manager.

WAITRESS (Walks back in and down to Gary) The chef says you can have chips on their own. It's 90p a plate.

GARY: That's all right by me. Could I see the manager please?

WAITRESS: What's the problem?

MICHAEL: It's nothing much really. We just mentioned to the lads over there that there was no smoking and they started to get abusive.

DECKO: Call the bleedin' manager if you like. We don't care. We're leaving lads, aren't we. (Decko stands up)

WAITRESS: You can't leave without paying for your pot of tea.

STEVE: I suppose you're going to make us, are ya? I'm getting out of this place. There's a smell off it anyway. (Steve stands)

OLD MAN: (Stands up) Nobody's leaving this restaurant until I say so.

WAITRESS: Oh Sir! I didn't recognise you.

OLD MAN: That's right. I'm the owner of this place and I decided to come in disguise to see if the service and food was as good as I thought it was. Now, have any of young gentlemen anything to say?

DECKO: Ah, no. Not really. Do we fellas?

OLD MAN: In that case you can leave. After you've paid for the tea and the bun you ordered. The waitress will collect it from you at the door. (They all exit sheepishly) *(Waitress goes back to exit)*

 **Production Notes**

1. This play must be performed with a Dublin accent except for the Old Man and Michael and Gary.

2. Use the classroom furniture to set the scene of a café. Students not in the production could sit in the café as extras.

3. Some of the stage directions are written in italics. They are based on the use of a stage plan (p. 16). These refer to specific movements the actors should make on the stage. They are not normally written into a script. It is the rôle of a director to supply a script with these movements.

## Drama Activities

Describe how you would dress:
- (a) the Old Man
- (b) the Waitress
- (c) any one of the young men.

Divide the class in two. Each group should allocate parts, read them through, learn off the lines for homework and put on a production in the classroom.

## Questions

1. Describe the gang of three in your own words.
2. How are the boys caught out in the end?
3. If you were acting the part, how would you interpret the character, Darren?
4. As a Director, what instructions about dress, accent and mannerisms would you give your actors to help highlight the difference between the two sets of young men?
5. What is the theme of the play?

## Writing Assignments

Write a café scene with three characters using one of the following ideas:
1. A customer complains to the waitress that the food is badly cooked. The waitress gets the manager. A discussion between the manager and the customer follows.
2. Two people eat a meal and when it is time to go home they discover they have no money. They decide to (a) run out, or (b) explain what has happened.

# Odd One Out

## CHARACTERS

Tony .........*A bully*
Gary (Gareth) .........*A bright student*
Karen .........*Student*
Lisa .........*Student*
Stephen .........*Student*
Paul .........*Student*
Miss Delaney .........*English Teacher*
Miss Richardson .........*Geography Teacher*

## Setting

The play takes place in a classroom. There is a row of desks at the back and down one side. The teacher's desk is at the other side. The play opens with Miss Delaney and her restless class, working.

TONY: Can I read, Miss?

KAREN: I like this story. I read it before.

TONY: So what if you read it before. Nobody cares!

STEPHEN: I care. Don't I Karen? I care.

KAREN: Oh shut up Stephen. I'll read Miss. Nobody else is as good as me. Tell them to be quiet, Miss.

MISS DELANEY: You're not reading Karen. Tony is.

TONY: See, I told you. She wants me to read.

GARY: I'll read Miss. That will shut them all up. (He grins)

MISS DELANEY: Later on, Gareth.

LISA: Let him read Miss. He's good.

MISS DELANEY: Right. Gareth, start the story.

GARY: (Apologetically) I'm not sure I like it.

MISS DELANEY: Read!

GARY: (Reads for a few lines, then stops) It's not my kind of story Miss. I'd prefer not to continue with it. (There is a knock at the door)

GARY: There's a knock at the door Miss. Will I answer it? (The class start to make noise)

MISS DELANEY: (Patiently) Just go on with the story.

GARY: I'd prefer not to, Miss. Can somebody else read?

MISS DELANEY: Gary, what's the real problem?

GARY: I'd rather not say Miss.

STEPHEN: He's chicken.

LISA: Leave Gary alone.

GARY: See Miss. It's no use.

MISS DELANEY: There's something going on here and I'm going to get to the bottom of it. (The end of class bell rings) Read that story and answer the questions on it everyone for your homework. (The class stand up and start to get ready to go. Miss Delaney shouts.) Put your chairs back into your desks and leave quietly! I expect to see homework from everyone tomorrow. Including you Gareth!

GARY: (Grins pleasantly) Yes Miss. Of course. Have I ever let you down?

TONY: (Mimics him) Have I ever let you down?

KAREN: There's more than you in the class you know, Gary. There's all the rest of us.

GARY: (Still grinning jokingly) You lot! You're nothing to my genius. Amn't I right Miss?

MISS DELANEY: I'll pretend I never heard that last remark. Now would everyone leave quietly. (They all start to leave)

KAREN: (at door) What about our trip to the mountains, Miss?

MISS DELANEY: We'll talk about that tomorrow. I haven't made all the arrangements.

KAREN: Right so Miss. I suppose I'd better be going (She calls out) Hey yous lot. Wait for me. I'm comin'! (She leaves. Shortly after, Sheila Richardson, a geography teacher, comes into the room).

# Class Acts

MISS RICHARDSON: God, what a day!

MISS DELANEY: Yes. I know what you mean. Roll on summer. There's a bit of trouble brewing with Three One (Third Years) I'm afraid.

MISS RICHARDSON: Oh! I thought they'd had enough warning.

MISS DELANEY: It's not that. It's Gareth. I'm afraid his classmates don't like him too much.

MISS RICHARDSON: Has anything in particular happened?

MISS DELANEY: No, but he's not as friendly as he used to be. It's almost as if he's decided not to draw attention to himself. He wouldn't read a story for me today for instance. I think he might be being bullied.

MISS RICHARDSON: It's a pity – he's so bright. It's just drawing attention to himself and he *can* sound a bit arrogant when he's talking.

MISS DELANEY: I might have a talk with the Principal about it in the morning. (Gary comes back into the room)

GARY: Hello Miss Richardson. I didn't expect to see both of you here. I hope I'm not interrupting.

MISS DELANEY: That's alright Gareth. What brings you back?

GARY: I just came to see if you had my copy and what you thought of my poem.

MISS RICHARDSON: I'll be off. We'll talk about that matter again when we have more time. Goodbye Gary.

GARY: Goodbye Miss Richardson.

MISS DELANEY: Goodbye Sheila. (Miss Richardson exits. Miss Delaney hands Gary his copy) Gareth, is there something going on that I don't know about? For instance, why did you really not want to read today?

GARY: (Shrugs his shoulders) I don't know. It's just that I don't think they want me to. That's all.

MISS DELANEY: Who are "they"?

GARY: You know. The lads. Tony and Stephen and Paul. But I don't mind Miss. Honestly. I'm all right.

# Odd One Out

MISS DELANEY: Have they been getting at you?

GARY: A little – (Pause) Not much – (Pause) I can't stay. I have to go to my next class. You can tell me what you thought of the poem later. See you Miss. Bye.

MISS DELANEY: Bye Gareth. (He leaves. She puts some copies into her bag and leaves the classroom also. Later Karen and Lisa come into the room. Karen beckons to Lisa and calls her over to Gareth's desk. She searches this and begins to look through the others)

LISA: What are you looking for?

KAREN: I told you. It must be here somewhere.

LISA: It's only a note.

KAREN: I know. But if the teacher saw it…

LISA: You're only trying to protect Tony. That's all.

KAREN: I'm not. Gary is an awful eejit anyway. He deserves everything he gets.

LISA: I know he's a bit of a lick. But that's no excuse to beat him up. (There is a knock at the door. The person tries the handle and then goes away)

KAREN: Oh me heart!

LISA: We'd better get out of here.

KAREN (Still searching) Wait a minute. Here it is. It's signed by Tony, Stephen and Paul.

LISA: Paul? I thought he was Gary's friend. Some friend!

KAREN: Here. You mind it. We'd better get out of here before the teacher gets back.

LISA: I don't want it.

KAREN: OK. I'll put it in the bin. (She does)

LISA: Right. Let's go. Come on. The bell is going to go. If anybody asks us what we're doing we'll say we're collecting the class register… (She takes this out of her bag to show it)

KAREN: Good idea. (She fixes a few desks. Lisa helps her. They exit)

(Miss Delaney enters. She starts to tidy her desk. Putting something in the bin she finds a note. She reads it. Gary knocks on the door. She puts the note in her drawer. He comes in)

GARY: I'm sorry to disturb you Miss, but I have a few minutes and I thought I'd come back and collect my poem.

MISS DELANEY: Of course Gareth. I have it here. But before I discuss it I want to talk about something else.

GARY: Oh. Is anything the matter? It's not about something I've said, is it?

MISS DELANEY: No Gareth. Well at least, not exactly. (She hands him the note) Do you know anything about this? (He reads)

GARY: If this really is true, maybe you should be talking to the people who wrote it. If you wouldn't mind Miss, I'd like to bring this home to show it to my parents.

MISS DELANEY: Leave it with me Gareth, and I'll look into it. In fact, I'm going down to show it to the Principal this moment.

GARY: If you do that Miss, they'll get me on the way home from school.

MISS DELANEY: It doesn't work like that Gary. We have some control over these matters in the school. Trust me and the matter will be dealt with right away.

GARY: I hope you're right Miss. Is Miss Richardson taking us today for Geography?

MISS DELANEY: Yes she is. She should be here any minute now. You wait here until she arrives. Just sit at your desk and say nothing to the class if they come in before her. I'm going down with this note to the Principal. Don't say anything to anyone about this when they arrive.

GARY: No Miss. But I'd prefer if you let me handle it my way. (Teacher exits. Boys and girls come into the classroom. Four boys pass down by Gary on either side, pushing into him as they do. Finally, they knock against his chair and he falls off)

Gary: Hey fellas. Cut it out! I'll tell Miss Richardson what you're doing when she comes in.

STEPHEN: Lick. That's all you ever do. Lick up to the teachers. Isn't that right fellas?

TONY: Don't hurt Gary's feelings. It might not be good for his brains to have to cope with it. I suppose you think your brains are better than anyone else's, do you

Gary? Well I don't think much of them and neither does anyone else here. You're just a teacher's lick, trying to make the rest of us look stupid.

STEPHEN: Give us your glasses Gary! (He grabs Gary's glasses)

LISA: Give him back his glasses Stephen.

TONY: Look at him now! He's as blind as a bat. Throw them here Stephen.

STEPHEN: Here Paul, catch. (He feigns throwing them at Paul, but throws them at Tony instead)

LISA: Tell them to stop Karen. Tell them to stop what they are doing. It's not fair. Gary didn't ask for any of this!

KAREN: Gary is just a swot. He's getting what's coming to him.

LISA: Tony, give them to me!

TONY: If you want them catch them. (He throws the glasses and they fall at Lisa's feet and break)

LISA: Now look what you've all done. I'm sorry Gary.

GARY: (Runs and picks up the glasses. He shouts at the class) You stupid crowd of ignorant pigs! I suppose this is what you think is good fun! Well I can tell you one thing – I'm not coming back into this class or this school ever again, and no amount of begging on any teacher's part is going to make me. You're all just a pack of cowards. I'll go to a school where at least what I do will be appreciated. The problem about you lot is you wouldn't know how to use your brains, even if you had them. I hope you all stay ignorant and stupid for ever. (He picks up his bag and storms out)

## Production Notes

1. This play is about twenty minutes long. It takes place in a classroom. When on stage, make sure that the speaking actors are in a position to be seen by the audience at all times. This is particularly important in the argument scene at the end of the play.

2. This play was written with students of a Dublin school in mind. You can use their accent or adapt it to your own. Gary might speak a little differently.

3. Though the students might be in uniform their individuality can come out in

their hairstyles, shoes and so on. Gary would be neat, and with short hair, for example.

4. Pay particular attention to the stage movements needed at the end of the play when Gary sits down after Miss Richardson leaves the classroom.

5. The character of the class is a noisy inattentive one. There can be no noise when an actor is speaking but the students can show their inattentiveness in other ways, by lounging or turning around or chewing gum.

##  Drama Activities

1. Read the play through twice.

2. Write what you think the stage movements for the play would be, in pencil, into your script.

3. Cast the play. Those without speaking parts can be extras in the classroom.

4. With or without scripts, ask one of the students to direct the play using their pencilled in stage movements.

5. Divide the class into groups and get them to work on their own plays based on the following ideas.

   (a) Two students are bullying another. A third student comes along and saves the one who is being bullied. (Four students)

   (b) Two students complains to the teacher in the classroom that another student hasn't got her homework done. The latter takes it up afterwards with the girl who complained. (Two students)

   (c) A student is accused of talking during a test. Her test is taken up. She had completed her test at the time and was talking about something else. She goes to the teacher to explain this. What does the teacher do? (Two students)

   (d) One student sees another take money from a schoolbag in the classroom. He speaks to this student and tells him what he saw. The student denies it. The boy talks about it to a friend. The student whose money was stolen tells the teacher. He also tells the teacher he thinks it was stolen by the boy sitting beside him because this boy was talking about money he had found and how he was going to spend it.

The teacher interviews the boy with the money. The boy denies stealing it. The teacher sends him down to the headmaster.

The two boys who know who stole the money talk about what has happened. The one who saw the money being stolen now tells this to the teacher.

The teacher calls in the student who stole the money and questions him until he admits his guilt. He is told he is suspended until he brings in his parents.

Finally the headmaster conducts an interview with the guilty boy in the presence of his parents, the boy who saw the money being stolen and their teacher. (Ten students)

(e) A student is being bullied by another student. She goes to her teacher and complains about what is happening. (Two students)

(f) Two students on the phone to each other plan on staying away from school the following day. The mother of one of the students bumps into them in a shop the following morning. (Three students)

(g) A student gets a bad report from school. Conversation between this student and her parent. (Two students)

 **Writing Assignments**

1. Who is your favourite character in this play and why?

2. In what way is Gary the "Odd One Out"?

3. This play is about bullying in school and its effects on a student. How does this bullying work and what is seen to be its consequence? (Quote from the play.)

4. Write out the dialogue from the piece you acted in or another sketch on a similar theme.

5. Write a story on one of the following:
   (a) The school bully.
   (b) Success at last.
   (c) A school outing.

# The Kiss of Life

### CHARACTERS

Queenie Buxom
Pearl Wisdom
Hairdresser
Manicurist
Agent
Bouncer
Begger
Secretary
Doctor Mendhearts
Voice of Newsreader

Sewage workers:
Blake
Broken
Bright Dreams
Biff
Brick
Bungle
Bad sight

## Scene 1

Scene opens in Queenie's room. She is before her mirror. She is having her nails done. She is also having her hair styled. Secretary is at her desk. Agent is at the filing cabinet.

QUEENIE: (To hairdresser, looking in mirror) Oh, you stupid fool. Look what you've done to my hair! I have to get it right for the beauty contest. One more mistake and you're fired!

HAIRDRESSER: I'm very sorry Queenie. You're still very important though.

QUEENIE: Jackass! (To manicurist) Be careful. Let me see my nails. Oh my Gosh! I asked for pink, not red. Get out of my sight at once! (To hairdresser) You too, you're fired. Get out immediately!

SECRETARY: Queenie, I have a lunch invitation here from the President. Do you want to attend?

QUEENIE: Is it actually signed by the President himself?

SECRETARY: No, his secretary.

QUEENIE: Write back and say I can't go unless the President signs the invitation. What are you staring at? Get to work.

# The Kiss of Life

SECRETARY: Certainly Queenie. Whatever you say.

BEGGAR: (Knocks on door. Bouncer answers it) I'm selling tickets for the Association of the Blind. Would anyone like to buy?

BOUNCER: (Putting hand in his pocket) How much are they?

QUEENIE: What's going on here? Who is this creature?

BEGGAR: I'm selling tickets for the blind.

QUEENIE: Liar. You're probably up here to spy on me! I'm not a rich person you know! How much do you want, five dollars? Well you can't have it. Now get out before you're thrown out.

BOUNCER: You heard her buddy. Beat it!

BEGGAR: All right. I'm going.

QUEENIE: (To agent) Scanlan. Come here at once. (She picks up mirror)

AGENT: Yes, Queenie?

QUEENIE: Am I or am I not the most beautiful person in the world?

AGENT: You are. Of course you are.

QUEENIE: Look. Here I am from another angle. Amn't I stunning?

AGENT: Yes. Very beautiful. But...

QUEENIE: No buts. I'm just perfect.

AGENT: But there is a rumour going around about someone else.

QUEENIE: Rumour. What rumour?

AGENT: (He appears to be fending off blow) That there is someone more beautiful than you.

QUEENIE: It's a lie! I don't believe it! Help, somebody. Call the doctor. I'm going to faint!

AGENT: Oh my God! Look what I've done now. (Fusses about) She'll fire me too. Quick somebody. Call a doctor.

SECRETARY: I'll call the doctor. (Phones) Dr Mendhearts? Come to the penthouse

## Class Acts

flat, Washington Buildings, Washington Street straight away. There's someone dying.

QUEENIE: (Sitting up) Dying! Who's dying? I'm not dying. But somebody will be if she's not found. I have to win the Miss Delight beauty contest. I'm the best! Do you all hear me? The best!

PEARL: (Walks in the door) Oh, I'm sorry. I thought this was the Ladies.

AGENT: It's her. It's the beautiful Pearl everybody is talking about.

QUEENIE: Trap her. I want her alive. She won't get out of my clutches. Come here Missy. Come to Queenie.

DOCTOR: (Arriving) Is this where the patient is? I got a call to say someone was dying.

QUEENIE: What's going on here? Does nobody ever listen to me? Get that man out of here!

PEARL: He was only trying to help!

QUEENIE: Nonsense! You little fool! How dare you contradict me. I can't stand people who contradict me. Bouncer. Bring in the dogs!

DOCTOR: (Takes a long syringe out of his bag) As long as I'm here nobody will hurt this lady. (Takes Pearl by the arm) Let's back out. Gradually does it. Nobody come near us until we're down the stairs. (They exit)

QUEENIE: (To Bouncer) After them. I'll get that pair if it's the last thing I do. Nobody can do this to Queenie and get away with it. You fools – after her! (They all exit)

## Scene 2

This scene takes place in the front room of the sewage workers' flat. It contains a door, window, couch, television set and anything else considered suitable.

When the scene opens Pearl is standing at the door listening to the voices of Queenie and Bouncer outside. A dog barks.

# The Kiss of Life

QUEENIE: (From off-stage) Get her. Where is she? Tramp. We're coming to get you!

BOUNCER: She's disappeared! She's got away!

QUEENIE: You stupid fool! You're fired! All of you! You're all fired! (Voices fade away)

PEARL: (Looking around) Where am I, I wonder? I've never been in such a poor house as this before. I'd better not look outside to see what has happened to the doctor. Maybe if I ask the people who live here if I could stay for a while, Queenie Buxom might forget about wanting to get me, dead or alive. I could study for my exams from here and enter for the Beauty Contest at the last minute. All I want to do now though is fall asleep. (She turns on the television, sits on the couch to watch and falls asleep. There is some recorded music at first then the music for the News comes on. We hear the voice of the announcer)

NEWSREADER: This is the news, read by.....(student's name) Queenie Buxom, twice winner of the Miss Delight beauty contest, is offering a reward of £1,000 to anyone who can provide information on the whereabouts of Pearl Wisdom, now tipped as the favourite for this year's contest. Miss Buxom is quoted as saying "she would like to see a fair contest". Anyone with this information can get in touch with Queenie Buxom herself or ring us here at 041-7318933. (Pause) Hello. Yes. Yes. I can take a phone call. Who is this on the line? You have sighted Pearl Wisdom in your area? We'll pass on your news to Queenie Buxom straight away. Well, that was a good start. Let's hope they're successful. And now for the rest of the news..... (He continues to read the news, meanwhile the seven sewage workers enter)

BAD SIGHT: Oh, I'm so cold and tired. I wish it wasn't my turn to cook the dinner.

BLAKE: What's this? Someone's left the television on again. (He turns it off and then sees Pearl) Everybody look! Look everybody, see who's here! (They all gather round the couch)

BURN: She's beautiful.

BRICK: She's probably lost.

BROKEN: I'll put the kettle on for tea. She might be thirsty when she wakes up. (He starts to tip-toe away. As he does so it is apparent he has a hump on his back.)

BRIGHT DREAMS: I'll get a blanket. (He starts to move)

## Class Acts

BUNGLE: She'll be frightened when she wakes up and sees us. I'll get her a Teddy. (He pauses when Blake speaks)

BIFF: Sshh...She's stirring.

PEARL: Where am I?

BRICK: In the house of some sewage workers of New York city.

PEARL: Couldn't you get a better job?

BIFF: The pay is good and somebody needs to do it. Who are you?

PEARL: Pearl Wisdom. I'm sorry for coming into your house. The door was open and I was being chased and now I need somewhere to stay for just a while.

BRIGHT DREAMS: Sure you can stay. How can we help you out? Are you being chased by bad people?

PEARL: Yes. Queenie Buxom. She wants to kill me.

BAD SIGHT: We could dye your hair and get you some new clothes to wear.

PEARL: What I would really like would be my medicine books to study.

BRICK: I can see to that. What's your address?

PEARL: Apartment 5, over Luigi's drugstore, 42nd Street.

BRICK: Your wish is my command. (He gets up and goes out)

BUNGLE: The best we can do now is leave you to rest. We'll go into the kitchen and prepare a meal. Does everyone agree? (They all nod their heads) In the meantime, if anyone calls to the door don't answer it. We'll have something nice for you to eat in just a jiffy.

BRIGHT DREAMS: O.K. everybody. Let's go. I'll wash the breakfast dishes.

BROKEN: I have this most delicious recipe called Superman Stir Fry.

BLAKE: I have to make the beds. (They all exit)

PEARL: Oh, I'm so tired. (She falls asleep. After a few moments Bright Dreams comes back in with a blanket and puts it on her. He dims the lights (if possible). He exits. A few seconds later Queenie puts her head in the door)

QUEENIE: Ah, there she is. So, my information was correct. The so-called beautiful

Pearl Wisdom herself. She won't be very beautiful when I finish with her. (She comes in the door and looks around. She goes down the stage, puts a bag on the floor and starts to look in it) This is just the job for my bag of tricks! (She rumages in the bag and pulls out a toy snake) What have we here? A deadly snake. Looks just like a pretty necklace to me. A deadly necklace. Ha ha! Nobody stands in Queenie Buxom's way and gets away with it! (She moves towards the couch) Now charming snake, do your work and Kill Kill Kill! We'll see who wins the Miss Delight contest after this. (She places the necklace on Pearl's neck and leaves. Pearl sits up and struggles as though trying to remove the snake and then falls as if dead)

BUNGLE: (At door) Dinner time, young lady. (Pause) She really must be tired. I'll have to go and wake her. (He picks up a hand bell and shakes it gently in her ear) Wakey, wakey pretty lady. Pretty lady what's the matter? (Shouts) Blake, Broken, Bad Sight, Bright Dreams, everyone come here quickly, our visitor is dead. (They all rush out. Broken goes back for a First Aid kit)

BROKEN: Out of the way everyone. (They all move back. He sees the snake and removes it)

PEARL: What is it? Where am I? I had a terrible nightmare! I dreamt I was dead! It was awful.

BRIGHT DREAMS: Count your lucky stars you're not dead. Severe measures are called for if we're to protect you. We will have to board up the windows and lock all the doors. We have learnt our lesson. The evil murdering person who is trying to get you must not be allowed find a way into this house in the future.

# Scene 3

The scene is the same as Scene 2. The stage is empty. Pearl comes on reading a book aloud.

PEARL: There are two hundred and twenty-six bones in the body. The main ones are, the back-bone, the clavicle, the ribs, the femur...Oh my God, I'll never learn all this and my exams are next month! I wish I could have just a little more time.

BLAKE: (Comes in with tray) Breakfast Poppet. I made tea and toast for two. We can have it together.

## Class Acts

PEARL: Oh, thank you very much Blake. (She sits down at table and starts to eat) Mmm. Very tasty. I hope I don't put on weight.

BRICK: (Comes in, lifting weights) Did someone mention the word weight? Time for your daily exercise routine Pearl.

PEARL: Not now Brick. Not while I'm eating my breakfast.

BRICK: O.K. See you later. (Smiles) Mmm. Breakfast. What a good idea. (He exits, lifting weights)

BROKEN: (When he enters on stage his hump is more apparent. He comes up to Pearl and looks at her as though from below) Is my beauty ready for a jaunt around the room, up and down the stairs and through the bedrooms? Up on my back quickly. It's just the thing for a good start to the day. Gives the brains a rest, this early in the morning.

PEARL: Oh, not now Broken. In a minute. You're all so kind to me. I have to eat my breakfast.

BROKEN: Whatever you say Beauty. Your wish is my command. (He goes out, singing)

Pearl sits at the table with her back to the side entrance. Bright Dreams comes in carrying a rose. Blake follows carrying a cake. He motions to those who are coming after to be quiet. They all enter. When they are all in Blake signals. They all start to sing. "Happy Birthday to you, Happy Birthday to you, etc."

PEARL: (Turns around) Oh. This is amazing! How did you know it was my birthday? Oh it doesn't matter! I'm so happy! This is the happiest day of my life! I don't know how to thank you all. (She kisses each one) Thank you Blake and Broken and Bright Dreams and Brick, Biff and Bungle and Bad Sight. I wish I could repay you all in some way. (There's a knock on the door. A plastic bucket of water has been strategically placed over the door, ready to fall on whoever enters)

PEARL: Oh my Gosh, there's a knock on the door! It's her again. (They all listen) Maybe this time our plan will work and she'll be the one to be caught out. Hide everyone, quickly. (The workers all dive into various hiding places. Pearl calls out loudly) Come in! (The doctor comes in. The bucket empties on him)

DOCTOR: Oh my goodness, what's this? I thought this was the door to the Men's room.

# The Kiss of Life

PEARL: (Rushes over to him) I'm sorry. I'm so very sorry. It's the doctor who rescued me from Queenie Buxom isn't it? What are you doing here?

DOCTOR: I've just moved into the flat upstairs. I don't know how it is we keep meeting like this. Could I have a towel please?

PEARL: Certainly. Of course. I'll get it.

BLAKE: No Pearl. I'll get it. (All the workers repeat the offer to get it in their own way. No I'll get it, Leave it to me, etc. They all exit)

PEARL: I'm so sorry. Really I am.

DOCTOR: I'll be alright. Don't worry about me. (Each of the workers rushes back in with a towel. The doctor's bleep rings. One of the workers rushes to him with a mobile phone. He dials)

DOCTOR: Hello. Is this the hospital? Dr. Mendhearts here. Yes. A baby delivery? Certainly, yes. Address please? I'll be there right away. (He puts the phone away) I've got to go on a call. See you all later. (He exits)

PEARL: (Calls from the door) What about the towel? (The workers shake their heads and exit) Oh well, time for study. Well, at least I know I have a new neighbour. (She puts on her walkman and sits down)

BLAKE: We're off to work now Pearl. Don't forget not to open the door to anyone. Your present won't be delivered. We'll be home late, even so, we'll bring you a nice treat for your birthday.

PEARL: Yes, Blake.

BLAKE: Did you hear me?

PEARL: Of course I did. Now you're late as it is. You'd better get to work straight away. I promise I won't leave today. I've so much work to do before this evening, I couldn't anyway. See you later, Blake.

BLAKE: Bye Pearl. (He gives her a kiss. All the workers come out and exit, saying and waving goodbye)

PEARL: (Takes off walkman) Now what was it Blake said? I'm having your present delivered today because it will be too late this evening. Or, whatever you do don't open the door until your present arrives this evening? Whichever it is I'd better be very careful. (She hears a knock on the door) This is unexpected. I don't think anything could arrive this early in the morning. I'd better look first before I open the door. (She looks out a spy hole or opens the door slightly and closes it again) It must be my present. It's somebody with a tray of doughnuts. I suppose I'll see what's happening.

QUEENIE: Hello, young lady. I'm from the Good-Food Doughnut Company and we're offering samples of our doughnuts as a sales promotion. Would you like to try one? I'd especially recommend this one with the raspberry centre. (She points it out).

PEARL: Promoting doughnuts? Oh, I thought this was my birthday present. Certainly I'd like to try one. (She picks one from the tray) I think I will have the raspberry centre. (She takes a bite, swallows, holds her neck as if in pain and falls as though dead on the floor)

QUEENIE: Ha ha! I got you this time, you little schemer. Nobody will stop Queenie from winning the beauty contest now. Look at you, as dead as a poisoned sewage rat. That's the end of your chances. It's Queenie Buxom all the way. Winner three times in a row of the world Miss Delight beauty contest. (She exits laughing, forgetting to bring her tray with her. There is a long pause)

The voices of the workers can be heard outside the door, laughing and talking. Bright Dreams calls out, "Pearl we're home! Open up! It's your friends, the workers." There is no reply. Broken is heard to say, "She must be asleep. We'll go in quietly". He opens the door and sees her.

BROKEN: Oh my gosh! Look what's happened! (They all rush in)

BLAKE: Poor Pearl!

BIFF: Call a doctor someone!

BRICK: (Lifts her hand for pulse) There is no pulse.

BAD SIGHT: She's still as beautiful as ever.

BRIGHT DREAMS: Sweet dreams, my darling Pearl. Sweet dreams, forever. (He cries)

BUNGLE: Don't cry, Bright Dreams. Something will happen to bring her back. I'm sure of it. (He goes to the phone and dials) Hello, is this the doctor upstairs? Is your name Dr Mendhearts? Fine. We have a patient here who seems to be dead. (They all cry) It's the girl in the flat below you. Could you call down straight away? Thank you. (Almost as soon as he puts the phone down the doctor arrives)

# The Kiss of Life

DOCTOR: I came at once. How is she?

BRIGHT EYES: Very beautiful, doctor.

BROKEN: She won't take rides on my back anymore.

DOCTOR: Clear the way and let me see. (He lifts her hand) What is her name?

BUNGLE: Pearl.

DOCTOR: Beautiful Pearl. What she needs now is the kiss of life. (He kisses her. She wakes)

PEARL: Oh Doctor. my dream has come true. I've been dreaming, it seems forever, that you would take me in your arms and kiss me.

DOCTOR: I love you Pearl. You are the most beautiful Pearl I have ever seen. Will you marry me?

PEARL: Yes, dear Doctor. The answer is yes with all my heart. (They embrace. The workers cheer)

BIFF: What's this? (He lifts up the tray)

DOCTOR: Let me see it. Yes, I recognise this. Yes, there's a name on it. Queenie Buxom. I saw it before in her apartment. She's the one who is afraid Pearl might beat her in the Miss Delight beauty contest. Even if she denies it, I'm sure we could trace her fingerprints from it. (He looks around) And here is a piece of doughnut. If I get it analysed it will show traces of poison. All we'll need then is a blood sample from Pearl to match it up. Fingerprints on a tray and a poisoned doughnut. With this evidence it looks as if Queenie Buxom won't be winning the next Miss Delight beauty contest now or for a very long time.

BLAKE: Three cheers for the doctor and our beautiful Pearl. Hip hip, hooray, etc.

PEARL: And now I'd like to say a word of thanks to the seven kind workers, all of you my friends who took me into your home without a question and then into your hearts. I am very grateful. With the money I win you won't have to go to work any more. The doctor and I will get married. I'll buy a big mansion, you'll come and stay with us and we will all live happily ever after!

Class Acts

 **Production Notes**

1. This play has two different settings:
   A. Scene 1 – A room in Queenie Buxom's flat.
   B. Scenes 2 and 3 – The front room in the flat of the sewage workers.
   When designing your stage make sure that where you position the furniture does not block the audience's view of the characters or action on stage.

2. Pre-recording the Newsreader's Item: The following points must be taken into account.
   A. The introductory music to the news and the voice of the newsreader must appear to be as authentic as possible.
   B. Pre-recorded news items are normally operated off-stage by a student allocated to this task.

3. Personal Props
   All actors have to be responsible for their own personal props. For example, Queenie Buxom needs a snake necklace, doughnuts and so on.

4. Voices Off-stage
   Characters talking off-stage must be loud enough to be heard and yet remain hidden from the audience.

 **Drama Activities**

1. Allocate parts and read the play through twice in the classroom.
2. Make a list of the stage furniture needed and draw plans to show where these are positioned in the two different settings.
3. Put the characters on these set plans by using numbers to show where they would be sitting or standing when the curtain rises at the beginning of each scene.
4. Make a list of Queenie Buxom's personal props and, where applicable, the personal props of the other characters.
5. Decide the costumes the characters are going to wear and make a list of these; Queenie Buxom requires a number of different costumes.
6. Learn off as much of the play as you can and act it out in the classroom.
7. The play "The Kiss of Life" is a modern version of the fairy tale "Snow White and the Seven Dwarfs". Read the following scenario for a similar type play based on the fairy tale "Little Red Riding Hood." When you have finished reading it write out or act out one or all of the scenes from this play.

# The Wolf

## Act 1

A gang of criminals whose leader is "The Wolf" have been terrorising the neighbourhood. The main place they attack unsuspecting passers-by is a local wood which people from the outskirts of the town often use as a way to the shops.

The granny of a girl called Rachel lives at the other side of this wood. Rachel has always been told never to use the wood to visit her Granny. Everyone, especially her mother, is aware of how dangerous this could be.

One day Granny rings up Rachel's mother and complains that she is not well. "Will Rachel go to the Post Office and collect my pension?" she asks. "Of course," Rachel's mother agrees and calls Rachel in from playing to explain what has happened. "I want you to bring some of my home-made bread and a cake to Granny also," Rachel's mother explains, "but whatever you do don't go into the wood...." "I'm not that stupid!" exclaims Rachel, highly indignant that her mother should accuse her of this and she snatches up her bag and leaves the kitchen without listening any further.

## Act 2

This scene opens with Rachel sitting on a stone, front stage left. There are trees behind her and a road at the edge of the stage which she is following. She is tired. She yawns and stretches her arms as if they are sore.

Another person comes on stage. It is The Wolf. He is nicely dressed and pretends to be mannerly. He stands beside Rachel, takes out some sandwiches and offers her one. She refuses. He offers her a sweet. She takes it. He asks her why she is tired. She explains that she has walked from the town with a message from her mother and still has a long way to go. He suggests that it might be easier to go through the wood. She starts to explain that she isn't allowed but when she turns to him again he has disappeared.

She searches all around for him and eventually goes into the wood. While she is in there she calls out, "Hello! Where are you? Where are you Mister?" He comes out; and takes the rock she has been sitting on (polystyrene boulder) and places it at the other side of the stage. He is sitting on this when she comes out of the wood. "I've been looking all over for you," she exclaims. She becomes confused because she cannot now make out from which direction she has come. The Wolf questions her about where she is going and why. In her confusion Rachel tells him everything including who she is and her Granny's address. He sends her away from where she would normally find her Granny's house.

## Act 3  Interior of Granny's House

Granny is tidying up. There is a bed in the centre of the stage. She hears a knock at the door and asks "Who is it?" "Rachel, it's Rachel," the Wolf replies. "Come in," Granny calls. There is no reply. The Wolf has crept round to the window. Granny goes to the door to see who is there. The Wolf jumps lightly in the window and picks some jewellery off her press. She comes back from the door. He grabs her from behind before she can see him and tells her he is going to lock her in the cupboard so that she cannot identify him.

He does this. Just as he is about to leave by the window he hears another knock at the door. It is Rachel. He grabs some of Granny's bed-clothes and a shawl for his head and puts them on and hops into bed. When Rachel comes in she apologises for being late and explains what has happened. The usual fairy-tale like conversation takes place between Rachel and the bogus Granny in the bed. Her final, "Oh Granny what sharp teeth you've got," is answered by The Wolf taking out a knife – "Not as sharp as the blade of this to chop you up with," he yells and jumps out of the bed. He chases Rachel. She screams. Dad, who is a policeman, arrives at the door and chases The Wolf. He eventually disarms him and arrests him. Granny calls out from the cupboard. They set her free. Rachel asks her father how he happened to be so close to Granny's house and hear her screams. He tells her that he had been patrolling the area for a long time on the look-out for a dangerous criminal called The Wolf. He describes him. The Wolf is still wearing Granny's night-clothes and they have not recognised him. Just then Granny cries out, "That thief is wearing my best shawl" and grabs it off him. They all recognise who it is. The father tells Rachel that though she should not have gone into the woods everything has worked out well. She and Granny have been saved and the neighbourhood is now rid of its most dangerous criminal, The Wolf.

# The Wolf

## ✒ Writing Assignments

1. In the play "The Kiss of Life" give your interpretation of the characters: a) Pearl Wisdom and b) Queenie Buxom, under the following headings (i) appearance (ii) personality (iii) relationship with the other characters.

2. Name a piece of music or a song you would like to use to begin and end this play. Explain your choice.

3. (i) Two characters exit from the stage almost as soon as the play begins. Who are they?
   (ii) Where on the stage is Queenie at this time? (e.g. downstage right, etc.)
   (iii) How can you position Queenie to let the audience know that Queenie is the most important person on the stage in the first scene?
   (iv) Mention the first thing she says or does that shows the audience she is not a very nice person.

4. Where must Pearl stand when she walks in the door of Queenie's flat to make sure she is seen by the audience? (Show this by drawing a simple plan)

5. From the time Pearl comes on stage until the end of the first scene at what point do you think Queenie stands up?

6. (i) What kind of expression is on Pearl's face when she comes into Queenie's flat?
   (ii) What other emotions does she express before the end of the first scene?

7. How is Pearl feeling at the beginning of Scene 2?

8. When the sewage workers first come on stage how can you ensure they do not see Pearl until the television is turned off?

9. Pearl is not just beautiful but clever as well. How do we know this?

10. The lights go down before Queenie comes on stage in Scene 2 and the atmosphere changes. How does Queenie look and act to contribute to this change of atmosphere?

11. Describe the appearance of the workers as you would imagine them on stage. Use their names to help you in your suggestions.

12. The atmosphere on stage is a happy one at the beginning of Scene 3. How does the appearance and actions of the workers contribute to this atmosphere?

12. (i) At what point in the scene does the atmosphere change?
    (ii) Who is the first to cry?
    (iii) Draw a stage plan to show where the other workers are standing when Bungle phones the doctor.

13. The character of the doctor has not much depth. If you were acting how would you portray this part?

14. What is the theme of the play?

15. Pick another fairy-tale you know. Write as a play story-line with a modern setting.
    **or**
    Write a story, a poem or a prose essay called "Friends".

# A First Confession

A Play for Schools, adapted from the story – *A First Confession*

### CHARACTERS
Jackie ......... *a young boy*
Nora ......... *his sister*
Granny
Priest 1
Priest 2 ......... *played by the same or different people*
Mrs Walsh ......... *School Teacher*
Priest's Visitor
The Devil
Children in the classroom

Scene 1. A kitchen in Cork City (1950's)
Scene 2. A classroom
Scene 3. Inside a church

## Scene 1 (In the Kitchen)

Granny comes into the kitchen. She is wearing a black shawl and carrying a pair of boots in her hands. She is also wearing a long black dress. Her hair is in a bun. When she comes on stage she is singing *The Banks of my own lovely Lee,* or something similar. She puts the boots down by the fire.

GRANNY: There now, that should keep them warm for me. Sure the Bishop of Cork himself wouldn't have as good a fire. (She fixes the fire) Be the Lord God, all this hard work would put a great thirst on you. (She straightens up) Maybe there's a dropeen of porter left in the press. I'll go and see. (She walks over to the press at the other side of the stage, takes a jug of porter and a glass, drinks and wipes her mouth with the back of her hand) Oh, the devil is in it. (Pause) Sure what's the harm. Your only auld once. (She puts the porter back in the press) Maybe now I could have a bite to eat. That's if I could have a go at cooking the spuds and sausages. (She goes to the door of the kitchen and calls out) Nora, Nora, have you eara notion where the sausages are for the dinner? (Nora is upstairs)

page 49

# Class Acts

NORA: I left them in the press for you, Granny.

GRANNY: Right so. I'll get them and put them on to cook. Let you come down here to help me.

NORA: I'll be down in a minute, Granny.

(Granny starts to sing again. She takes the sausages out of the press. She puts these into a saucepan. She takes some potatoes out of a bag, and puts these, without washing them, in on top of the sausages. She pours water on the lot)

GRANNY: Be the holy now, there's a meal fit for a king. (She goes over and puts the saucepan on the fire. She takes the boots from the hob and puts them on the kitchen table) They should be warm enough by now. Maybe I'll have another sup of porter. (She goes to the press. Nora comes into the room. She has pigtails and is fat. She is wearing a uniform. As soon as Granny sees Nora she puts away the porter in a hurry, so that the girl doesn't notice)

GRANNY: Nora, that wasn't long you spent upstairs. I thought you were supposed to change your uniform.

NORA: Sure there's no rush. I'll change it later.

GRANNY: You'd better. Before your Mammy comes home.

NORA: What's for dinner? (She smells the air suspiciously)

GRANNY: Spuds and sausages. (Nora goes to the fire to see. She lifts the pot lid and holds her nose. (Granny wipes her mouth to hide the evidence) Is there any sign of that brother of yours?

NORA: I have no idea where he is. He was supposed to come home with me. He must have got kept back as usual. The little caffler. He has his last Communion class with Mrs Walsh this afternoon too. He's making his first confession tomorrow. First confession how are ya! That fellow has so many sins on his soul, he wouldn't know how to confess them. (Noise at door) That's probably him at the door now. (The door opens and Jackie comes in. He is small. His hair is cut very short. He is wearing short trousers. He is younger than Nora. He puts his schoolbag on the table. Granny lays the table)

NORA: Well, what kept ya? (Jackie pretends he doesn't hear. He puts his tongue out at her behind her back and helps Granny lay the table. He takes the boots off but Granny puts them back in the centre of the table again) I said where were you? You're very late. Granny has your dinner ready.

# A First Confession

JACKIE: It's none of your business.

NORA: Granny, did you hear that?

GRANNY: Sure he doesn't mean it, the wee chap. Sit down here and have yer dinner. (She brings the saucepan over to the table. They reluctantly sit down. Granny puts her dinner out and brings it over to the fire. She puts the plate on the hob) Salt. Why did I forget the salt? It must be old age. (She goes to the press and pours herself out a glass of porter. Nora gets up and puts her dinner in a bucket while this is happening)

JACKIE: Granny!

GRANNY: (Still at the press, her back turned) What is it now?

JACKIE: Nora's after throwing her dinner away.

NORA: Liar!

JACKIE: I am not, Granny, come and see.

GRANNY: (Finishing porter) Are you two ever goin' to stop fighting? (She turns to the table) Well, isn't she a marvellous girl. Nora, you've finished your dinner entirely. That deserves a penny. And what about Jackie?

JACKIE: If she doesn't eat hers, I'm not eating mine. (He stands up to put the dinner in the bucket. Nora grabs him and pushes him back down)

NORA: I'll make him eat it, Granny. The dirty little caffler. Here, give me that (She grabs the spoon out of his hand and tries to force-feed him. Jackie struggles. In the process the dinner gets thrown over Granny's boots)

GRANNY: (Takes up the boots and starts to clean them off with her apron) Now look what you did, wicked boy. That's the last dinner I'll ever cook for you. Ruined my good boots that I haven't even worn this past year or more to keep them new. Wait 'til your mother comes home and you'll hear more about this. Where's me stick until I hit him a belt.

NORA: Go on Granny, get him. He deserves it. I'll hold him for you. (She tries to grab Jackie. He lifts up a breadknife from the table)

JACKIE: Keep away! Keep away from me the pair of ye. If ya come near me again I'll stick this in ya. (He gets under the table) Now, see if you can get me.

## Class Acts

GRANNY: Mother of God, he's a murderer!

NORA: Granny, I'm all sore from Jackie. My arms and legs are paining all over. Look at him now. I'll have to get out of here before he kills me. (Pause) Can I go down to the post-office to get your pension?

GRANNY: This is a terrible state of affairs. That boy will turn into a bad lot if he's not careful. (She goes to the press and takes out a pension book. She also takes out the empty jug for porter) Here girl. Do as you said and run and get my pension for me. Take a shilling for yourself for sweets. You deserve it. Go quickly now before he strikes at you. I'm not staying with him another minute! (She shakes her fist at him) This is not the last you'll hear of what has happened young man, if I have any say in it. I'll be back later to deal with you. (They both exit. Nora gesticulates silently at Jackie before she leaves)

JACKIE: (Coming out from under the table) That sister of mine would turn anyone into a murderer. If Granny wasn't living here in the first place none of this would have happened. I'm done for anyway. I can't stop committing sins and tomorrow I have to make my first confession. What I need is some advice. (Pause) Oh – I nearly forgot. Mrs Walsh will be waiting to give her last first communion class. (He grabs his bag and exits)

## Scene 2 (A classroom)

The set is a normal classroom. An average of twelve students can be used. These are to include Jackie, the student who'll play the priest and the student playing the devil. Props include students' desks, a teacher's desk and a candle. The students are at their desks when the scene opens. The teacher walks into the room.

MRS WALSH: Good afternoon everyone.

ALL: Good afternoon Mrs Walsh.

MRS WALSH: Open your catechisms and leave them on the desks before you. Pay attention. (Class settles down) What is confession all about? (Pause) It is about telling your sins. Today you are going to learn what will happen if you don't tell all your sins to the priest. Does anyone in the class know what will happen? (Pause. Nobody answers. They are not paying very much attention) If you don't tell all your sins then you will have made a bad confession. Repeat after me. If you don't tell all your sins you will have made a bad confession.

# A First Confession

CLASS: (Repeats) If you don't etc..

MRS WALSH: Exactly. Very good. There is a terrible place people go to if they don't tell all their sins. Can somebody here tell me where that place is? Jackie O'Connor?

JACKIE: Hell, Mrs Walsh.

MRS WALSH: Right. I asked you because you're not paying attention. (She addresses the class) Stop talking. Once more please. What does hell look like?

JACKIE: It's hot Mrs Walsh. (Class laughs)

MRS WALSH: I said looks like, not feels like, dunderhead. Anybody else?

STUDENT (Who is also priest puts her hand up) Please Mrs Walsh, it feels hot and it looks like a red-hot furnace.

MRS WALSH: Very good answer. Remember what you've been told and listen in future, Mr O'Connor. Now I am going to conduct a small experiment. Get up from your desks all of you. Quietly. Move in around me, at the sides here where everyone can see. (She arranges the class around the sides of her desk) Can you all see?

CLASS: Yes, Mrs Walsh.

MRS WALSH: Pay attention! (She takes a candle out of a desk drawer and puts it on the desk. She opens her purse and takes a coin out. She shows these items to the class) Stop fidgeting there at the back! I'm only going to do this once. Watch me closely. Are you watching Jackie O'Connor?

JACKIE: (Pushed from behind) Yes Mrs Walsh.

MRS WALSH: You had better be. (She picks up the candle and the money) In my right hand, boys and girls, I have a candle. In my left I am holding a half a crown. I will light the candle. (She lights the candle) This money is for anyone who is willing to put their finger onto the flame of this candle here for five minutes. Only five little minutes. Because if you can hold your finger on the flame then you will know how hot hell is. Any volunteers? (She brings the candle close up to people in the class. They shrink back) No? I thought not. Back to your places everyone please. (They all go back to their places) Now fold your arms, put them on the desk. Close your eyes and listen. (She paces up and down the classroom) Think of the pain. Think of sitting on red hot coals and not being able to get off them. You can open your eyes now. (She goes up to her desk and puts out the candle and puts it away).

## Class Acts

Stop talking. It's time for our little play. Those in charge get ready. Everybody help. Get the desks in order. Jackie, tell us all what this play is called. (Students lift desks and move them quietly)

JACKIE: The bad confession, Miss.

MRS WALSH: Louder.

JACKIE: (Shouts) The bad confession.

MRS WALSH: Keep your voice down Jackie O'Connor! We're not deaf in here. Are the group involved ready?

PLAY GROUP: Yes, Miss.

MRS WALSH: Quiet everyone else! A sweet for everyone if this goes well. (Pause) What do you say?

CLASS: Thank you, Mrs Walsh. (The stage is now ready for the classroom play. All the desks have been moved to one side. The students not involved become the audience. A bed, made from three chairs, is in the middle of the floor. The priest is asleep on the bed. He is covered by a sheet. The audience is quiet. The play begins. The priest snores. A visitor arrives. He approaches the priest and pokes him in the back).

PRIEST: (Jumps up). What? What is it? Who's there? What's the matter?

VISITOR: It's only me.

PRIEST: What do you mean, it's only you? Who are you? How did you get in? What are you doing here?

VISITOR: I'm very sorry for disturbing you. I...I...(Pause).

PRIEST: Oh, this is ridiculous! I haven't got all night. Get on with what you have to say.

VISITOR: (Kneels down and clutches the priest's sheet. The priest is now sitting up) I want to make a confession father.

PRIEST: (Starts to lie down again) What, at this hour? I'm too tired. Come back again in the morning.

VISITOR: It can't wait, Father. I haven't been able to sleep night or day because of a weight on my mind.

# A First Confession

PRIEST: (Still lying down, with his eyes closed) All right. What did you do that's so bad?

VISITOR: It's only that, the last time I went to a priest I forgot to tell one sin. I made a bad confession. It's been haunting me ever since!

PRIEST: (Stands up) Well in that case my son, because it is so serious, I will help you out. Wait here until I get what I need. (He goes out. The visitor sits down on the bed and pretends to sleep. The devil comes in. Eerie music starts to play. The devil does a circus routine with the man on the chair, pretending he is a ghost and involving the entire audience. In the end, the devil chases the man out. The devil comes back and leaves a placard behind him reading: THE DEVIL WAS HERE. The priest comes back in. He searches everywhere for the visitor. Eventually, he finds the placard. He reads it out loud) THE DEVIL WAS HERE (He shakes his head in wonderment) Well, that's marvellous, absolutely wonderful. Isn't it a fright what can happen in your bedroom. THE DEVIL WAS HERE. (He puts the placard down and starts to get excited) The devil. Oh my God! What am I going to do? I'll have to tell the Bishop. Say Mass. Talk to the parish priest. (He calls) Fr Doyle! No. I'll say nothing. People will blame me. They'll say I invited him in. I'll lose my job. Just because a man made a bad confession. This is terrible. (He calls out) Fr Doyle! Fr Doyle! (He rushes from the room)

MRS WALSH: (Steps onto the floor) Come out the actors and take a bow. (They bow) A round of applause everyone. (The rest of the class clap) Good. Very well done. A sweet for all tomorrow. Fix the desks. Quickly. No talking.

JACKIE: (Puts up his hand) Mrs Walsh.

MRS WALSH: What is it?

JACKIE: You left your 2/6 pence on the desk.

MRS WALSH: So I did. Thank you very much Jackie. (She puts it in her bag) Quiet class. One more word. Remember the message of the play. God is watching you. Examine your conscience. Good luck tomorrow!

JACKIE: Did you see that?

STUDENT: What?

JACKIE: The way she took the 2/6 pence.

STUDENT: I did. I was led to believe a person as close to God as her didn't need money.

JACKIE: There's something wrong somewhere. (He shakes his head)

STUDENT: Have you all your sins ready for tomorrow?

JACKIE: That's my problem. I can't remember them all. And when I do I keep committing more.

STUDENT: There's no hope for you so. You can't escape it. You're a sinner. Whatever you say tomorrow, you'll still be making a bad confession. (Exit)

## Scene 3 (Outside and inside a church)

Nora is seen dragging Jackie along, up the side or through the audience towards the stage. She talks to him in a very bossy tone, telling him to hurry up, typical of him, everybody else has been there for ages. What will the priest say? She's ashamed to be seen going into the church with him so late, no other girl she knows has a brother as bold as him. The priest will probably refuse to have anything to do with him anyway because he has too many sins to tell, etc. They reach the edge of the stage.

NORA: Straighten yourself up and look respectable.

JACKIE: I'm alright. There's nothing wrong with me.

NORA: Let me fix your tie. (She re-knots it. She takes out her handkerchief) Spit on that. (She cleans his face with the wetted handkerchief. He struggles) Don't forget to tell the priest all your sins.

JACKIE: Leave me alone.

NORA: Go on inside now. I'll be waiting for you when you finish. (She pushes him in. Jackie stumbles then straightens himself up. He looks about him apprehensively. Nora goes in after him and kneels with her face to the wall at the side of the stage. She does not move during this part of the scene. The priest is visible to the audience on the stage, he is sitting on a chair with his sideface to the audience. The confessional has no walls. The area it occupies on the stage is marked out by an oblong piece of material, a carpet, a piece of canvas, or something similar and is big enough to allow the chair and the priest to fit comfortably. At the right side of this is a lectern, with a shelf, high enough to be above the seated priest's head and strong enough for Jackie to climb on. The priest's head is bowed. When Jackie first approaches the confessional he kneels on the wrong side. He knocks on an imaginary wall as if to listen)

# A First Confession

JACKIE: Bless me father. (Pause. Priest stands up from his chair and mimes listening)

PRIEST: Yes, my child.

JACKIE: (Moves to another wall. He shouts) Bless me father.

PRIEST: (Shouts) Is there somebody there? (At the same wall as Jackie)

JACKIE: (At third wall) Bless me father for I have sinned....

PRIEST: (Moved to third wall) If there is somebody there would they please show themselves!

JACKIE: (Moves to the fourth wall and climbs up on the lectern. He balances on this so that he is looking downwards at the priest through his legs, as if hanging upside down) Bless me father for I have sinned, this is my first confession.

PRIEST: (He twists his head upwards as if he has stuck it through an opening to see who it is. He shouts angrily) Come down from up there! (Jackie tumbles down from the lectern dramatically and rolls well away from the confessional. Nora hears the noise. She is positioned so that her back is to Jackie. She stands up, sees him and stamps her foot in annoyance. She strides over.)

NORA: (She grabs Jackie) Jackie, what is the meaning of this? I might have known something would happen. Disgracing me like this. You little caffler. (She stretches to hit him. He catches her hand. They fight. The priest steps out and separates them)

PRIEST: (He pushes Nora off Jackie) What's all this about. Who are you? If you're the boy's sister, you can't treat him in this way, you little vixen. It's an absolute disgrace.

NORA: I am his sister. (Whimpers) I can't do my penance with him, Father.

PRIEST: Can't do my penance! Get away from here or I'll give you more and then we'll see how you feel. (Nora turns and walks away. She leaves the stage at the front but stays just outside it. Priest watches. He lifts Jackie up by the arm) What's your name young man?

JACKIE: Jackie, Father. Thanks for helping me out.

PRIEST: Don't mention it. It's a wonder to God she didn't hurt you badly. Are you here to make your first confession?

JACKIE: Yes, Father.

# Class Acts

PRIEST: You're late you know.

JACKIE: I'm sorry father.

PRIEST: You must have committed a terrible sin to stop you from coming.

JACKIE: I did, Father.

PRIEST: Well, tell me about it. Tell me about it.

JACKIE: I don't know how to say it. (He paces up and down) I've been wanting for a long time now to kill my grandmother.

PRIEST: (Starts to pace up as well) I see. I see. This is a serious matter. I suppose you plan to cut the body up in pieces and take it away in a wheelbarrow?

JACKIE: Well Father, I don't know. I hadn't thought about it. But that's not all. There was something else as well. I tried to kill my sister with a breadknife.

PRIEST: Is that the sister who was beating you up outside?

JACKIE: (Miserably) 'Tis father.

PRIEST: Someone will go for her with a breadknife some day, and he won't miss her. You must have great courage. Between ourselves, there are a lot of people I'd like to do the same to but I haven't got the nerve. Hanging is an awful death.

JACKIE: (Coming closer) Is it Father? I was always very keen on hanging. Did you ever see a fellow hanged?

PRIEST: Dozens of them. And they all died roaring.

JACKIE: (Shaking his head in disbelief) Jay!

PRIEST: Would you like a sweet? (He takes a bag out of his pocket and offers one to Jackie)

JACKIE: (Takes one) Thanks, Father.

PRIEST: Have them all. Go on, you might as well. (He gives the bag to Jackie) Come in to the box and tell me more. (They both take their places in silence and mime conversation)

(Nora comes on the stage. She walks around the church for a while looking for Jackie. She approaches the confessional and whispers loudly) Jackie if you're in there, listen to me. I'm not waiting for you any longer, just because you have so

# A First Confession

many sins to tell. Come out now or I'm going home. (She leaves the stage and waits again outside)

PRIEST: So, is that it now Jackie?

JACKIE: Yes, Father. You know, you've taken a great weight off my mind. For the past while I've been thinking I was going to burn in hell forever.

PRIEST: No fear of it. If that was to happen to you, what hope would there be for the rest of us. Bless you Jackie. And now in the name of God, we'll both leave. (The priest blesses the boy. They rise to exit.)

JACKIE: Thank you Father. (They shake hands)

PRIEST: Goodbye Jackie. (They part, the priest exits backstage)

JACKIE: (Waves) Goodbye, Father. (He walks out to where Nora is sitting)

NORA: So you decided to come out at last. It's about time. I suppose the priest had to get rid of you!

JACKIE: No. As a matter of fact I wasn't put out. I walked out. And the priest walked out with me.

NORA: The priest walked out with you! That's a good one. I suppose you'll be saying next he gave you no penance.

JACKIE: He didn't, or hardly any. (Jackie takes out the bag of sweets and starts to eat one)

NORA: What's that you've got?

JACKIE: Sweets. What else? Want one?

NORA: I do not. I expect you're going to say now they belong to the priest and he gave them to you.

JACKIE: Of course. That's just what happened.

NORA: Well that beats all. You try and kill me. I get given out to and you get sweets. It doesn't make sense!

JACKIE: I know. You'll just have to face up to it. Follow my example. You'd be better off being a sinner after all. (Puts another sweet in his mouth and walks off)

Class Acts

 ## Production Notes

1. This play is set around 1950 in Cork city. It has three scene changes.
   (a) A simple old fashioned kitchen.
   (b) A classroom of that time.
   (c) A church interior.

2. Costumes and props should be in-keeping with the period.

3. If you are performing this play on a real stage, dimming of lights would be very effective to create a ghostly atmosphere for the "devil episode" of the classroom scene.

4. By using extras in the classroom scene, the entire class can be involved in this production.

 ## Drama Activities

1. Make a list of the large and small props needed for the three scenes of the play.

2. Describe the clothes (a) Jackie, (b) Nora, (c) Granny could wear in the first scene.

3. Draw plans of the three stage sets, showing where you would put the furniture on each set and an entrance/exit.

4. Read the following stage movements for the opening of Scene 2. *Mrs. Walsh walks into the room from a door at backstage right. She walks across the room to her desk at front stage left. The class stop talking and stand up. Mrs. Walsh sits down. The class sits down.* Now write the stage directions describing Granny's movements from the moment she appears on stage at the beginning of the play until Nora enters.

5. Allocate parts and read the play through twice.

7. Cast and perform any one scene of the play.

 ## Writing Assignments

1. Draw a plan to indicate the position of the three characters on stage when Jackie dives under the table with the bread-knife.

# A First Confession

2. If you were acting the part of Nora, what tone of voice would you use towards (a) Granny, (b) Jackie, (c) the priest?

3. Pick out what you think is the funniest episode in the play, describe what happens and say why you think it is funny.

4. Describe what you think would be the most difficult piece of this play to stage. Give reasons for your answer.

5. Pretend you are Nora. Now write, in your own words, your opinion of Jackie. In the same way write Jackie's opinion of Nora.

6. If you were given the part of Granny to act how best do you think you would do it to bring out her character for the audience?

## ? Questions

1. On what story is this play based and who wrote it?

2. Read the story and discuss any similarities and differences between it and the play.

3. Describe the plot of the play in your own words.

4. What, in your opinion, is the theme of the play?

5. Pick out your favourite part of the play and say why you like it.

6. Nora is in a stronger position than Jackie at the beginning of the play but by the end their roles are reversed. How does this happen?

7. Humour is one of the main ingredients of this play. Would you agree with this statement? If so, quote or describe incidents from the play to prove your answer.

8. Write an essay or poem on one of the following?
    (a) Family.
    (b) Star of the show.
    (c) Wrongly accused.
    (d) The Tramp.

# Not My Best Friend

### CHARACTERS
Jackie .........  } *teenagers*
Tanya .........
Geraldine ......... *sister of Jackie*
Mrs Ferguson. ......... *mother of Jackie and Geraldine*

## Scene 1 (Girl's Bedroom)

Two girls both aged 13-14 are sitting on two single beds in a girl's bedroom. Both are eating sweets and reading magazines. The girl, Tanya, closes her magazine, stands up and puts it down. She goes over to Jackie's bed and takes a sweet from a packet. She stretches and yawns and goes down front stage. Jackie has earphones on and is listening to music.

TANYA: Gosh, I'm so bored. I wish I had something to do. If Rebecca had come along we might have had a bit of fun. (Pause) Did you hear me Jackie?

JACKIE: (Takes off earphones) What did you say Tanya?

TANYA: Oh forget about it. It doesn't matter.

(She starts to fit some of Jackie's clothes over hers before the mirror)

TANYA: I got £50 for my birthday last week. Of course a lot of it is gone. How much are you going to get?

JACKIE: I don't know, £10 maybe. It's not until Saturday week.

TANYA: (Sarcastically) Oh, lucky you. (Pause) Listen Jackie, I know what we'll do. We'll go into town tomorrow. You know, bunk off school and I'll spend the rest of my money. I could even lend you some if you want.

JACKIE: This is a bit sudden. Tomorrow. I don't know. Maybe. I'll have to see.

TANYA: What do you mean, you'll see! Sure nobody will notice you've done it. There's so much trouble in your house anyway you'd get away with anything.

JACKIE: What do you mean?

TANYA: Well, you know. Your parents splitting up and all that. I'm sorry Jackie, but you know. (Silence) Ah, come on. It'll be a laugh. We'll meet Sharon and Rebecca.

JACKIE: I might not want to.

TANYA: You're a coward.

JACKIE: I am not.

TANYA: Well decide then.

JACKIE: (Pause) I'll give you a ring later on. (Looks at her watch. Stands up from her bed and puts away the magazine) I'd better put these away before Geraldine finds out. I'm not supposed to read them. You'd better go, Tanya. Don't forget you said you'd be home at six o'clock.

TANYA: What time is it?

JACKIE: Half five.

TANYA: Oh gosh! It's late. I have to go to my Granny's first for dinner. Mum won't be home until nine o'clock and then she and Dad are going out for a meal.

JACKIE: That's nice, I suppose.

TANYA: Of course it's nice. They've gone out three times this week and tomorrow we're going to have a Chinese take-away. I love King Prawn Fou-yong, don't you?

JACKIE: I don't know. I suppose so.

TANYA: What do you mean, you don't know! It's delicious! I've had all the Fou-yong dishes so far. Sometimes Dad lets me have two choices from the menu because it's too late to cook.

(Jackie starts to put school books in Tanya's bag)

TANYA: What are you doing?

JACKIE: I'm just tidying up your books for you.

TANYA: Talk about dropping a hint! O.K. I'm going. I know when I'm not wanted.

JACKIE: It's not that. I thought you said you were in a hurry.

TANYA: (Sarcastically) Oh, come off it Jackie. I'll be off anyway, it's about time. (She picks up her bag)

(Voice off-stage) Jackie! Jackie! Do you hear me calling you?

## Class Acts

TANYA: That's your Mum. (Pause) She's coming up, I think.

JACKIE: It's Mum alright! It's probably to tell me dinner is ready. I have to help her lay the table.

MRS FERGUSON: (Comes in the door) Hello Tanya, you haven't left yet I see.

TANYA: Hi, Mrs Ferguson. I'm just about to now. By the way, Jackie and I had a piece of your chocolate cake if you don't mind. It was delicious.

MRS FERGUSON: That's all right Tanya, I told Jackie she could give you some. Have you arranged a lift home?

TANYA: (Putting her jacket on) I'll be O.K. I'll get the bus. I'm going to Granny's. She's got something planned for me. Something special to do. I don't know what. We might go to the pictures. (She picks up her bag) See you Jackie. Don't forget about our talk.

JACKIE: Bye Tanya. (Laughs. Tanya exits).

MRS FERGUSON: What was all that about, Jackie?

JACKIE: It doesn't matter. Just something... about the weekend... (Pause) Mum?

MRS FERGUSON: Yes. What is it?

JACKIE: You remember the ten pounds you said you were going to give me for my birthday. Could I have it a bit sooner...like this evening?

MRS FERGUSON: What's the rush all of a sudden?

JACKIE: Nothing. I just thought I'd go into town on Saturday.

MRS FERGUSON: I'll see then on Saturday morning. Now come on down and give me a hand. The chips are probably burning and you haven't done anything. (Mrs Ferguson exits)

(Jackie fixes the magazines a bit more. She exits)

## Scene 2 (The same room – some time later)

Some changes have been made to denote the passing of time, e.g. clothes on chairs or unmade beds, etc. Jackie comes in with her school bag. She throws it on the bed and goes over to her desk. She puts her cardigan or jacket on the back of the chair and sits down as if to settle down to work but then stands up and goes to the press and takes down a savings box. Her sister comes into the room)

GERALDINE: Hi, Jackie. Where's Mum?

JACKIE: I don't know. Is she not downstairs?

GERALDINE: No. She must have gone out for something.

JACKIE: She didn't say anything to me.

(Jackie puts her savings box on the table)

GERALDINE: What are you doing?

JACKIE: Nothing. Just counting my money.

GERALDINE: What for?

JACKIE: I'm going to buy some clothes on Saturday.

GERALDINE: Who with?

JACKIE: Tanya, if it's any of your business.

GERALDINE: Her! What are you going out with her for? She just uses you. You know that. Anyway you're supposed to be saving up to buy a guitar.

JACKIE: I've changed my mind about the guitar. Dad might buy me one for my birthday.

GERALDINE: You know he won't. He can't afford it. Anyway, you haven't enough money for clothes as far as I can see. (She picks a note off the table) What's this? Is this all you have, £5.

JACKIE: Leave it alone. (She snatches the money away)

GERALDINE: Have it your own way. I'm going down to the shop to get an apple. Do you want anything?

JACKIE: Will you get me a packet of popcorn please?

GERALDINE: O.K. Tell Mum I'm back if she comes in.

JACKIE: Maybe she did tell me she was going out and I didn't hear her.

GERALDINE: Fathead!

## Scene 3 (Inside a shop)

The set resembles a shop floor. There is a rack or two of clothes. A cashier at a cash desk, a few shoppers. Tanya and Jackie are in the shop.

TANYA: (She takes a dress down off one of the racks) Look at this Jackie. It's massive! I wonder how much it is?

JACKIE: Probably about £30. Let's see. (She looks at the tag) £10. It must be in a sale. It's nice, isn't it?

TANYA: Do you want to get it? I can lend you the money. My Dad gave me £40 extra last night for the shopping for the weekend. They're both going away. You can get it back from your Mum or your sister for me. You need some new clothes anyway.

JACKIE: What do you mean?

TANYA: You know. All the fellas! (She winks and starts to walk in an exaggerated fashion)

JACKIE: (Laughs) Yea, well maybe. (She puts the dress up to her) What do you think?

TANYA: You'd be a fool not to take it.

JACKIE: What do you mean?

TANYA: Take it...Buy it.

JACKIE: Oh. I thought for a minute you meant really take it.

TANYA: You wouldn't do that sort of thing anyway. I mean, good little Jackie. Teacher's pet. Butter wouldn't melt in her mouth. (Pause) Do you remember the time we were caught smoking in the toilets? (Laughs)

JACKIE: (Puts the dress up to her again) I might take it.

TANYA: You're only saying it!

JACKIE: Do you want to try me?

TANYA: Did you ever do it before? Steal something I mean.

JACKIE: No. But there's always a first time isn't there?

(A shopper comes towards them. They both turn towards the rack as if to look. The shopper goes away. Tanya holds out her bag)

TANYA: Here, put it in here. It's big enough. I'll put it on my shoulder on the way out. (Jackie puts the dress into the bag. They look about them and then saunter out)

## Scene 4

The sittingroom of the girls' home. Jackie and Geraldine are in the room. Geraldine is putting on make-up. Jackie is watching television.

GERALDINE: Did you have a good time in town today, Jackie?

JACKIE: What do you mean?

GERALDINE: You told me you were going into town today, remember?

JACKIE: Oh, you mean this morning. Sorry. Yes, I did.

GERALDINE: Did you buy anything with your £5.

JACKIE: Not much. I saw a lovely jacket and a pair of jeans but they were too dear. I just got a tee-shirt. Will I show it to you?

GERALDINE: Yes. You might as well.

JACKIE: It's mine now remember. You can't borrow it. I'll bring it down and show it to you. (She goes upstairs)

(Geraldine who has finished putting on her make-up starts to tidy up the room. She picks up a cushion and sees the dress underneath it. She picks it up and when she hears Jackie at the door puts it back. Jackie comes in. She is wearing the tee-shirt with a jacket over it)

JACKIE: (Making a trumpet sound loudly. Opens the jacket and shows off the tee-shirt as if modelling.)

GERALDINE: (With approval) Very nice Jackie. How much did that set you back?

JACKIE: £2. It's good isn't it!

GERALDINE: Yes, it sure is. I like the design on the front. Where did you get it?

JACKIE: The "Import Shop" in Geroge's Street. It came from Japan. They had a sale on.

## Class Acts

GERALDINE: I can see it has a Japanese look all right. By the way, is Tanya coming here tonight?

JACKIE: Yes, I think so. Why?

GERALDINE: Nothing. I just thought she might have left something behind her when she was here on Thursday. Did she say she was missing anything?

JACKIE: What sort of a thing?

GERALDINE: You know, clothes or anything.

JACKIE: What do you mean, clothes or anything?

GERALDINE: Nothing much. It's just that I found something she might have left behind under the armchair cushion. It's a dress. (She reaches in and lifts it out)

JACKIE: You've no right to be at that. Give it to me! It's mine.

GERALDINE: It looks nice. Where did you get it?

JACKIE: It's none of your business.

GERALDINE: (Looks at the price) £10. That's dear. I thought you had only £5 going into town.

JACKIE: It was only £5.

GERALDINE: The price here says £10. If you stole it you can say. I'm not going to tell anyone. It's just a bit stupid that's all. Suppose you were caught.

JACKIE: Well I wasn't.

GERALDINE: Mum will wonder where you got it.

JACKIE: I'm not going to tell her.

GERALDINE: She'll find out. You'd better put it away before she sees it. (She gives the dress to Jackie who starts to fold it and put it away. Her mother comes into the room. Jackie tries to hide the dress.)

MRS FERGUSON: What have you got there Jackie?

JACKIE: (Looks at the dress) This? Oh nothing. Just something I'm minding for Tanya. She got it in town this morning.

MRS FERGUSON: Is she staying here again tonight?

## Not My Best Friend

JACKIE: Yes. Her Dad is going to drop her off here at eight.

GERALDINE: Not again. That girl is never out of here. One of these days she'll move in altogether. It's bad enough having to share a room with one, not to mention two.

JACKIE: You have more friends over to stay than I have.

MRS FERGUSON: Stop fighting you two. Geraldine come out to the kitchen and help me put away the messages. Jackie, go up to your room and help tidy it. Your clothes are strewn all over the place. I won't be able to get as far as the bed next.

(Jackie picks up a book and pretends to read.)

MRS FERGUSON: Jackie, did you hear me?

JACKIE: I'm going. I'm going.

GERALDINE: Don't be cheeky to Mum. You were told to go up and tidy your bedroom. Now do it.

JACKIE: I'm going. O.K. There's no need to be so bossy about it. (She exits. Mrs Ferguson starts to tidy up)

GERALDINE: Sit down Mum and have a coffee. The messages will wait for a while. Relax. Put your feet up. You need a break. Watch television. There's a good programme on, "Hugh and Laurie".

MRS FERGUSON: I'm worried about Jackie as a matter of fact.

GERALDINE: She'll be alright. It's just a phase.

MRS FERGUSON: It's this separation. I'm afraid it's affected her badly.

GERALDINE: It's nothing to do with the separation, Mum. She's mixing with the wrong people that's all. Tanya only uses her. Did you ever hear her making fun of Jackie?

MRS FERGUSON: I know. I'll just have to keep a closer eye on her in future, and help her to try and get out of it. If I get the rest of the housework done now I could watch a film later. Is there anything good on?

GERALDINE: There's something on Network 2, I think. I'm going out at eight o'clock. Is that alright Mum?

## Class Acts

MRS FERGUSON: I suppose I shouldn't worry so much about Jackie. I'm just not happy with the way she is behaving recently. Anything could happen.

GERALDINE: Every marriage break-up causes problems. I'll put away the shopping for you now. I might watch "Star-trek" later. (They both exit)

(There is a knock at the door. This can be heard coming from off-stage)

JACKIE: Hi, Tanya. Come in. Why are you so early?

TANYA: I'm sorry. I hope your Mum doesn't mind. Dad had a meeting.

JACKIE: No. She won't mind. Come on into the sitting-room.

(They enter. Tanya is carrying a small bag)

JACKIE: Is that the only bag you have?

TANYA: Yes. It's enough until tomorrow.

JACKIE: Wait until I tell you Tanya. (Pause) You remember the dress? The one I took? Geraldine saw it and asked me where I got it and then Mum came in.

TANYA: What did you say to Geraldine? That you bought it I suppose.

JACKIE: No. I told her I took it, because she'd guess anyway.

TANYA: You said that to her? I wouldn't have the nerve. I'm glad I don't have a sister who gives out as much as her. How do you stand it?

JACKIE: (Airily) I just tell her to shut up. (Pause)

TANYA: And what did your Mum say?

JACKIE: When she asked me whose it was I said it was yours.

TANYA: Well that was clever. (Silence) I met Stephen when I was on the bus coming here.

JACKIE: (Pretending to be indifferent) Oh yes him! What did he say. Was he talking about me? (Laughs, but anxious)

TANYA: Yes. He said you'd be nice if it wasn't for the pimples on your face. (Pause)

JACKIE: (Obviously hurt but hiding it) Pimples, what pimples?

TANYA: Oh, it doesn't matter. It's only a joke. (She points to a press) Is that where your Mum keeps the Duty Free cigarettes? If you put a packet in your pocket now she wouldn't miss it and we could have a cigarette each later on. Did you ask your Mum about the disco tomorrow? It will be a laugh. Rory dropped a tab the last time he was there. He said he didn't know what happened for the next two hours. I don't know. I might try one. The two of us could try one if you like.

JACKIE: When? Tomorrow?

Tanya: Oh, forget about it. You're too afraid to do anything about it anyway.

(Pause. Mother comes into the room)

JACKIE: Hi, Mum!

MRS FERGUSON: Well Jackie, I see Tanya has arrived.

JACKIE: Yes. We're going up to my room first.

MRS FERGUSON: No, you're not. Not until you tidy it up.

TANYA: I'll help you. Come on Jackie. We might as well do it now. Sorry I'm early. I hope I'm not in the way.

MRS FERGUSON: That's all right Tanya. By the way, I was admiring the dress Jackie said you left behind.

TANYA: (Brightly) It is nice isn't it. I didn't tell Jackie but it's really hers. I bought it for her because she liked it so much. She can give me the money back later.

JACKIE: (Explosively) That's a lie!

TANYA: What? What's a lie? (She speaks innocently and smiles at Jackie as if she doesn't understand)

JACKIE: (Exasperatedly) Oh nothing!

TANYA: Jackie has great taste in clothes. She spotted that dress the first minute we went into the shop.

JACKIE: Tanya! (As if to say "don't lie")

TANYA: Come on. Own up Jackie. Admit you liked it. You'll be able to get the money back. Your father will probably give it to you when you go to stay with him next week, won't he Mrs Ferguson?

## Class Acts

MRS FERGUSON: Perhaps. But in the meantime I don't like to see you out of pocket money. You might need it for tomorrow.

TANYA: Who me? No, I'm alright. Honestly. Tell your Mum Jackie. It doesn't matter.

JACKIE: It was a sort of present Mum. Tanya doesn't mind. I'll pay her back myself some time.

MRS FERGUSON: £10 is a bit much to be paying somebody back. Next time you want a dress as expensive as that Jackie, let me know first please. You are due £10 for your birthday money next week. I'll give it to Tanya now and you can explain to your father what has happened.

JACKIE: But that's my birthday money!

MRS FERGUSON: (Takes some money out her pocket) Here Tanya. Now put it away and don't listen to Jackie when she says she likes a dress in the future.

JACKIE: What about you Mum? You might need the money yourself. You said you had to pay the milk bill or else we couldn't order any next week. Dad might not have that £10 for me for my birthday.

TANYA: Yes, it's alright I'm not in that much of a hurry Mrs Ferguson. Here have it back. (She hands the money back)

MRS FERGUSON: No. Take it. I insist.

TANYA: Well, if you do insist I suppose I'll have to take it. (She shrugs her shoulders) I'd better put it away safely.

JACKIE: Tanya! That's not fair, you shouldn't take that money from Mum.

TANYA: (Innocently) What? What's not fair? I said I didn't want it, didn't it?

JACKIE: (Angrily) You know what I'm taking about.

MRS FERGUSON: What's going on? (Long pause) There's more to this than meets the eye!

JACKIE: I'm sorry Mum. And there's more to Tanya than meets the eye, as well, it seems. I know I don't seen to be making sense Mum. I'm sorry as well if I've been behaving badly to you recently. I know things haven't been too good for the past few weeks and I haven't been a great help either. I wouldn't mind having a talk about all this. Maybe we could sit down and have a cup of tea later.

# Not My Best Friend

MUM: I think, in the circumstances, that would be a very good idea.

JACKIE: There's something else I'd like Mum. Could I sleep in your room tonight? I want to use the radio alarm to wake up early. I think I'll go to swimming in the morning.

MRS FERGUSON: What about Tanya? Are you going to let her sleep on her own?

JACKIE: Tanya can sleep in my room with Geraldine. Geraldine was asking me about the dress earlier and I told her exactly how Tanya and I got it. I'm sure she'd love to know about Tanya getting the £10 from you, Mum, because you wanted to pay her back early in case she had no money. Geraldine is always telling me how fond she is of Tanya, so that story will make her even more interested. (Pause) Can I go with Sally to a party tomorrow night Mum? It's being put on by the Youth Club. I have lots of friends there I have not met for ages. It's free. I'll just need to arrange for a lift home. Say I can go please Mum. I'll meet Sally at swimming and talk to her about it in the morning. (To Tanya) I'm sorry I won't be able to ge with you this weekend like you asked Tanya. I won't be free next weekend either. In fact, I can't see myself being free to go out with you for a long time in the future.

## Production Notes

1. The play requires three set changes. Apart from minor alterations, Scenes 1 and 2 are the same.

2. Actors must pay particular attention to pauses and silences. They should allow for a count of 3 approx. for a pause, and 5 for a silence. They are always a signal to the audience to pay attention to what is unsaid or left unspoken at that time.

3. The voice of the mother off-stage must be followed by footsteps to show she is coming up the stairs.

4. Extra actors will be needed for the shop scene.

## Drama Activities

1. Allocate parts and read the play through twice.

2. Draw stage plans for the three different sets.

## Class Acts

3. Learn off and act out the shop-lifting scene.

4. Place your characters on the stage plan for this set. When the scene opens remember the two girls must be able to hide themselves from the view of anybody else in the shop when shop-lifting.

5. Here are the stage moves for the shop scene:
   *The two girls stand downstage left.*
   *Shopper moves from backstage centre to downstage left and back again.*
   *Shopper moves to cashier downstage left.*
   *Girls exit backstage left.*
   *Now plan the stage moves for any other 30 lines of the play.*

 **Writing Assignments**

1. What is Jackie's attitude to (a) her mother (b) her sister (c) her friend, throughout the play?

2. Would you say Jackie is a typical teenager? Explain why.

3. Why in your opinion did Jackie steal the dress?

4. Why does she turn against her friend in the end?

5. What is the mother's main worry and what effect does she think this is having on her daughter's behaviour?

6. What is the older sister's opinion of Tanya? What is Geraldine's attitude towards (a) her mother (b) her sister.

7. What kind of a person is Tanya?

8. What tone of voice does Tanya use with (a) Jackie (b) Jackie's mother?

9. What is the theme of the play?

10. Write the following sets of dialogue:
    (i) Tanya and a friend at school the next day. Tanya is giving her version of what happened.
    (ii) Conversation between Jackie and her mother when Jackie tells her how she really got the dress.

Not My Best Friend

(iii) Conversation between two teenagers when one is telling the other about their parents separating.

(iv) Conversation between two girls about how they were caught shop-lifting.

# The Slumber Party

## CHARACTERS

Grace ......... *teenager*
Eileen ......... *friend*
Hazel ......... *friend*
Angela ......... *friend*
Mother (Mrs Condon) .........⎫
Father (Mr Condon) ......... ⎬ *Parents of Grace*
Sheila ......... *mother of Angela*
Betty ......... *mother of Eileen*
Mrs Hardcastle ......... *mother of Hazel*

---

The stage is dark. There is a noise of a chair falling over. A torch goes on and shines out to the audience.

EILEEN: Who was that?

ANGELA: Hazel.

EILEEN: (Points the torch at Hazel) Be quiet Hazel! We'll be heard upstairs!

HAZEL: (Pause) I'm sorry. Give me the torch. (She looks at her watch) Grace, it's two o'clock. You told me to tell you. It's time you agreed to drink whiskey for a dare.

GRACE: Thanks anyway Hazel. Eileen, you switch on the lamp. All of you get a cup each. Don't make any noise. I'll get the whiskey. (They all get a cup each)

EILEEN: I don't think we should do it Grace.

GRACE: I think you're afraid. But don't worry. We won't be found out. I'll fill up the bottle afterwards. If I was going to do it, you all said you would too. That was the agreement.

HAZEL: I hate the stuff. It's always around at home and I can take it whenever I like. Nobody would notice. My Dad threw out a bottle of English whiskey yesterday because he didn't like the taste.

GRACE: (Boasting) What a waste! He should have thrown it in my direction.

EILEEN: Show-off!

ANGELA: Are you sure we won't be found out? I'd never be let up here again if my parents were told.

GRACE: Just to make sure fraidy cat, I'll go into the hall and listen. (She tiptoes to the doorway and peers out) No sound. I'd better get some water from the kitchen to top up the bottle so that they don't notice what's been taken.

EILEEN: I suppose we'd better get on with this now that we agreed to it. Don't bother going into the kitchen. I have some water here in a bottle you can use. Hold on. (She takes it out of her bag)

GRACE: I'll get the whiskey… (She goes to the press and takes it out)

EILEEN: Can I have it Grace? I want to see what's written on the label. (She takes the bottle from Grace and reads) Power Gold Label 10 Year Old Irish Whiskey. Well, that doesn't tell us much.

ANGELA: (Innocently) What do you mean?

EILEEN: What the alcohol content is, stupid.

GRACE: (Takes back the bottle and reads) 40% proof. That's a lot. That's brilliant.

HAZEL: Whiskey is always 40% proof. I always read the labels.

GRACE: (Sarcastically) Oh! So Hazel's been raiding her Dad's cocktail cabinet again has she? Look, but don't touch.

HAZEL: (Offended) At least we have a cocktail cabinet.

GRACE: Not like some, you mean. (Putting on an accent) So we're mixing with the nobs now are we? Better be careful how we speak everyone.

EILEEN: Leave Hazel alone Grace.

ANGELA: My Mum and Dad lock everything away.

GRACE: I'm not surprised with you around.

EILEEN: (Interrupting) At it again.

ANGELA: (Ignoring this) What do you mean?

## Class Acts

GRACE: Oh, listen to her pretending. Oh, we know what you get up to Angela. We know!

EILEEN: For heaven's sake everyone. Stop arguing. Angela, collect the cups and bring them to the cupboard here. I'll measure the Whiskey out. Is the seal broken?

GRACE: Yes, Mum made an Irish coffee after dinner.

ANGELA: Did you bring the fags, Hazel?

HAZEL: We never agreed to have cigarettes.

GRACE: Angela, I can't believe it, you told me you never smoked a cigarette.

ANGELA: I didn't. But I can always try.

GRACE: Don't try here. You'll be coughing your head off.

HAZEL: Listen to the expert.

GRACE: I should know. I smoked five today!

HAZEL: (Sarcastically) That's the biggest lie I've every heard!

EILEEN: (Pours out the drink) Stop arguing and come and get your drink.

GRACE: No water for me please.

HAZEL: I won't have water either.

GRACE: Hazel, you've never drunk beer before, let alone whiskey.

HAZEL: So what!

GRACE: Well you're not going to drink it without water here. Not in my house. What will my parents say if you get sick. I do not want to clean up the mess.

HAZEL: There won't be a mess. I'll be alright.

GRACE: Well, please yourself. Don't say I didn't warn you. (They all pick up their drinks. Angela bumps into Hazel. She laughs)

EILEEN: Sshh girls. Keep the noise down.

ANGELA: Sorry.

HAZEL: It was your fault.

ANGELA: No it wasn't. It was yours.

## The Slumber Party

GRACE: Be quiet! (They all sit down) Well, down the hatch girls! (They all raise their glasses to their lips and react differently)

GRACE: Hmm. Delicious. (Pretending, in fact she doesn't drink it)

ANGELA: (Makes a distasteful face and lies) This is lovely. (She puts the drink down straight away.)

HAZEL: Whiskey is not my favourite drink.

EILEEN: Cheers everyone!

ANGELA: No thanks. I've had enough you can count me out.

HAZEL: It's disgusting.

GRACE: I never said you had to enjoy it did I?

EILEEN: Well that's one dare that didn't work. Give me your cups everyone and I'll bring them out to the kitchen and get rid of the evidence. Grace, you'd better top up the bottle with water for the morning.

## Scene 2

The same place the next morning. The floor has been cleared, sleeping bags are put away etc. Grace's mother Mrs Condon is continuing to tidy up when the doorbell rings. She goes to the door and opens it.

MRS CONDON: Sheila! Come in.

SHEILA: (Steps in) No, I couldn't possibly. I don't want to disturb. I just thought I'd call to see if Angela was ready.

MRS CONDON: They're all upstairs making the most of the last few minutes. Sit down. (Sheila sits. The doorbell rings again) Hold on a second. (She goes to the door again)

MRS HARDCASTLE: Is this number 15?

MRS CONDON: Yes it is. Mrs Hardcastle isn't it, Hazel's Mother?

MRS HARDCASTLE: That's right.

# Class Acts

MRS CONDON: Come inside a minute. The girls are almost ready.

MRS HARDCASTLE: It's Okay. I'm in a hurry. I'll wait in the car.

MRS CONDON: Certainly. I'll try and rush them up. (She calls up the stairs) Grace, hurry up there. The girls' mothers are waiting.

BETTY: (Steps in the door) Anyone home? Hello Ella, I see you've everything tidied up. Aren't you marvellous. I just called to see if Eileen was ready.

MRS CONDON: They should be down any second. They're impossible to get a move under. (Pause) I'll tell you what everyone, I made an Irish coffee for myself last night. We might as well treat ourselves to another. It won't last in this house very long.

BETTY: I know what you mean. That sounds like a lovely idea.

MRS CONDON: Would you like one, Sheila?

SHEILA: I don't want to put you to any trouble.

MRS CONDON: No trouble at all! (She goes to the press. Grace come to the door and sees this)

GRACE: Mum?

MRS CONDON: What is it, Grace?

GRACE: Nothing. (Pause) It's just that we're ready.

MRS CONDON: That's a pity. We were just about to have an Irish coffee. Some other time, perhaps. Still it's just as well I suppose. (The three girls come into the room) Everybody here?

EILEEN: Yes, Mrs Condon. We're all ready and thank you for having us. We've had a lovely evening. I hope we didn't make too much noise.

MRS CONDON: Well, even if you were a bit noisy at least I know nothing had been going on. That's one thing about having a party in your own house, you can keep an eye on the proceedings. (Pause) I've heard too many stories of drink at teenagers' parties recently. I feel I should be grateful for small mercies.

BETTY: That's true. It's very wise to try and avoid trouble. And they're such lovely girls too. (She looks at her watch) I suppose I'd better go. It's getting late. We'll be off. Eileen, say thank you to Mrs Condon for having you.

# The Slumber Party

EILEEN: I just did, Mum.

ANGELA: Thank you very much, Mrs Condon.

HAZEL: Yes, thanks. The whole thing was brilliant.

MRS CONDON: Not at all girls. My pleasure. You'd better go Hazel. Your mother is outside, waiting in the car.

SHEILA: I think we've overstayed our welcome. We'll all be going. Thank you again, Ella isn't it?

MRS CONDON: That's right. It's my pleasure. I'll see you all to the door. (They all exit. We can hear sounds of goodbyes off-stage.)

(Grace comes into the room. Takes the bottle of whiskey out of the press and is looking for a place to hide it when she hears her mother in the hall.)

MRS CONDON: (Outside) Grace, are you upstairs?

GRACE: (Hides the bottle behind the curtain) I'm in here Mum.

MRS CONDON: (Comes into the room to see Grace at the curtain) What are you doing?

GRACE: Nothing. I was just fixing the curtains. They weren't pulled back properly after last night. Are you going shopping this morning?

MRS CONDON: No, not until later on. Why do you ask?

GRACE: Nothing. It doesn't matter. (Silence) Mum?

MRS CONDON: What is it now?

GRACE: I lost my history book and I need one to study for my exams on Monday.

MRS CONDON: What are you trying to say?

GRACE: I have to get a new one.

MRS CONDON: I hope you're not expecting me to pay for it. You've had your party like you asked. I've spent all I'm going to on you for some time.

GRACE: Please, Mum.

MRS CONDON: Can't you borrow one? Or use your own pocket money to buy one. I'll give you the three weeks I owe you plus a week in advance. That should cover it. (Pause) Well, if you have nothing else to say I had better do the washing-up. I'll leave the drying for you when you get back from the bookshop.

GRACE: (Sullenly) I'm not going to the bookshop. It doesn't matter.

MRS CONDON: Please yourself if that's what you want. We might as well get started now. Come out with me to the kitchen.

GRACE: I'm coming. (They exit. A few seconds later Grace's father comes into the room. He sits down with his newspaper. He is reading for a few seconds when Grace comes back to collect some glasses)

GRACE: Hello Dad. I didn't know you were up.

DAD: I didn't get much of a chance to rest, did I? But it doesn't matter now. You all enjoyed yourselves last night I gather.

GRACE: Yes. We had a great time. (Pause) Dad?

DAD: Yes dear, what is it?

GRACE: Would you mind giving me a lift to the shops. I have to get something for school and I'm too tired to walk.

DAD: Is your Mum not going down?

GRACE: No. (She pauses before lying) She said you were.

DAD: Very well. But I'm not staying long. This is my day off remember. I want to watch the Ireland/Wales match.

GRACE: (Pleased) I just have to finish the washing-up and collect my money from Mum. I'll see you later. (After a moment Dad gets up and folds the paper. He puts it down beside a half-finished lemonade bottle. He looks at this and decides to put it in the press. He realises the whiskey bottle is missing. He calls Mrs Condon)

DAD: Ella, can you come in here for a moment please. There's something you might want to see.

MRS CONDON: (Comes to the door) What is it, love?

DAD: I did not want to say anything about this in front of Grace in case I'm not right but the whiskey bottle is missing.

MRS CONDON: Come off it! Let me look. (She looks) It's gone. You're right. I wonder what happened. I'll ask Grace. Maybe she knows.

# The Slumber Party

DAD: Is that wise? I mean something might have gone on last night we don't know about. It might not be a good idea to tackle it straight on.

MRS CONDON: Nothing could have gone on. Grace is only fourteen. She doesn't drink. There is some obvious explanation to this and we might as well find out. (She goes to the door) Grace, come in here for a minute please.

GRACE: I'm busy drying up.

MRS CONDON: It won't take a minute.

GRACE: (At the door) If it's about the bottle of whiskey, I can explain.

MRS CONDON: How did you know what we wanted you for?

GRACE: I guessed. That's all. It's behind the curtain. I hid it there because I spilled it last night and I wanted to replace it before you noticed it. (She goes to the window and picks up the bottle) I might as well throw it away.

MRS CONDON: Show it to me Grace! (She examines it) Why did you add water to it?

GRACE: So that you wouldn't see it was empty before I could buy a new one.

MRS CONDON: With the money you said you needed for a history book I suppose! It all sounds a bit fishy to me.

GRACE: It's true Mum. I'm sorry I lied about needing a book.

MRS CONDON: I hope it's the only thing you lied about.

GRACE: (Irritably) There's no need to give out. I said I'd replace it.

DAD: Calm down Grace. Nobody said anything about having to replace it.

MRS CONDON: Don't spoil her. She's had enough good things happen to her this weekend without you letting her off the hook entirely. She has to be made responsible for her actions.

DAD: What's happened has happened. Leave it to me and I'll sort it out.

MRS CONDON: Sort it out my foot! Find out would be more what I'd like it. This is not the end of it as far as I'm concerned. (Pause) Fair enough so. I'll be in the kitchen if you need me. (She leaves)

DAD: Look Grace. I'm aware accidents can happen but to spill a whole bottle of whiskey is a bit too much. You've seen how easily your mother can get upset. I know she has her suspicions but she can't say exactly what happened and we'll have to leave it at that. One way or the other you had no permission to touch any drink in the press.

GRACE: I'm sorry, Dad.

Dad: You know, of course, that it's going to have be replaced and that's your responsibility. I propose buying another bottle and keeping your money back every week until it's paid for.

GRACE: That's not fair. It wasn't all my fault.

DAD: Are you saying somebody else spilt it.

GRACE: No, but…

DAD: If you don't want to tell on your friends I can understand. I won't press the point.

GRACE: It isn't that. (Pause) Oh, it doesn't matter. Thanks anyway Dad.

(Pause. Grace's father starts to read the paper)

GRACE: Dad?

DAD: Yes, Grace. What is it?

GRACE: What if I really didn't spill the drink. What if my friends and I drank it?

DAD: Drink is a great temptation. I can understand somebody wanting to taste a drink just to see what it was like. If you did that I'd overlook it this time but it's not something I'd like to see you try and repeat. We all know about the dangers of teenage drinking and where it can lead to. My advice is to stay away from it for as long as you can, until you're old enough to drink it socially. Don't tamper with things that are too big for you to handle. Is that understood?

GRACE: I suppose so.

DAD: Now, how about the finishing the washing-up?

GRACE: Mum's done it by now.

Dad: (Good humouredly) I'm sure you'll find something to do to help her out. (He looks at her directly) After all, I'm going to clear up matters about the bottle of whiskey for you. I'm not going to say anything to your mother about the fact that you or your friends might have been experimenting with whiskey. All in all I don't think you have anything to complain about.

Grace: It's true Dad. I'm sorry. I will help Mum out and thank-you for not telling her about the whiskey. Even if I do have to pay for a new bottle I suppose I shouldn't give out. After all its not a bad sort of a bargain!

## Production Notes

1. The play is divided into two scenes. There are no set changes.
2. The stage is in darkness when the play opens. Stage lights come on when Eileen switches on the lamp.
3. The doorbell sounds will have to be pre-recorded and operated off-stage, unless you can wire up a doorbell for the actors.
4. Any voices off-stage must be loud enough to be heard by the audience.

## Drama Activities

1. Allocate parts and read the play twice.
2. Design a stage set, paying particular attention to where you put the whiskey press, the window and the exit.
3. "Grace: Thanks anyway Hazel. Eileen you switch on the lamp. All of you get a cup each. Don't make any noise. I'll get the whiskey. (They all get a cup each)" Find where this speech is at the beginning of the play. Place your actors by using numbers on the stage plan. Explain in writing what action you would direct each actor to do for the speech and in what directions they must move to complete their actions, e.g. upstage left, or front stage centre and so on.
4. (i) Plan the stage moves from the beginning of Scene two until the speech… "Mrs Condon: That's right. It's my pleasure. I'll see you all to the door." (They all exit. We can hear the sound of goodbyes off-stage)
   (ii) Now allocate parts, learn off this section and act it out for your class audience.
5. Make out a list of large and small props for the play, e.g. furniture, torch, whiskey bottle and so on.

6. Make a list of the characters. Beside each one give what you think is their predominant personality trait.

##  Questions

1. Discuss the personality of Grace. Quote from the play where possible.
2. What is Grace's relationship with (a) her mother (b) her father (c) her friends?
3. What role in the play would interest you most as an actor/actress? Explain why.
4. Pick out a speech in the play of your chosen character. Quote the speech and say what tone of voice you would use in acting it.
5. In what way would you dress the character of the father to show the kind of person he is? Explain your choice.
6. What is the theme of the play?
7. What was Mrs Condon's theory about having parties in the house? Would you agree with her argument?
8. How does Grace's father show himself to be an understanding person?
9. Who is the least likeable person in the play? Why do you say this? What type of voice would you use for this character?

## Writing Assignments

1. Write out the conversation that takes place between a parent and teenager on one of these themes:
   (i) Teenager asks to stay out late at a disco. Parent refuses.
   (ii) Teenager caught drinking/smoking by parent.
   (iii) Teenager refused pocket money for not doing housework.

2. Write a letter to the newspaper complaining about the bad press teenagers receive because of some teenagers drinking.

3. Write a short story, poem or prose essay on one of the following:
   (i) Parents.
   (ii) Friends.
   (iii) The Party.